MARRIAGE AND ITS MODERN CRISIS

Marriage and its Modern Crisis

Repairing Married Life

Alan Storkey

Hodder & Stoughton

LONDON SYDNEY AUCKLAND

British Library Cataloguing in Publication Data
Storkey, Alan, 1943–
Marriage and its Modern Crisis
1. Marriage   2. Marriage – Religious aspects
I Title
306.8'1

Library of Congress Cataloguing in Publication Data
Storkey, Alan
Marriage and its Modern Crisis/Alan Storkey
Bibliography: p includes index
1. Marriage – Sociology   2. Marriage – Christianity
I. Title
HQ 518

ISBN 0 340 67107 6

Printed and bound in Great Britain by
Cox & Wyman Ltd, Reading, Berks.

Hodder and Stoughton Ltd
A Division of Hodder Headline PLC
338 Euston Road
London NW1 3BH

To Elaine

The Potter centres us upon his wheel
and drives his knuckle in our heart
We turn, and yet his fingers hold us still
until we find we are his art.

CONTENTS

Preface   ix

1 Western marriage   1
2 Marriage in crisis?   19
3 A Christian understanding of marriage   35
4 Marriage and the families of origin   59
5 Friends, dating and mating   77
6 Cohabitation   92
7 Faith and marriage   106
8 Sex and marriage   118
9 Marriage and persons   129
10 Gender and marriage   139
11 The emotions of marriage   153
12 Marriage and work   164
13 Marriage and home life   174
14 The stages of marriage   182
15 Law and marriage   192
16 Marital breakdown and recovery   203
17 Marriage renewed   214

Bibliography   224

Index   237

PREFACE

The immediate context of this book is the increasing concern and debate over family issues in the media and politics in Britain and beyond. It is part of that debate and takes as its starting-point the understanding that there is a substantial crisis occurring in intimate relationships in the West. How substantial is open to discussion and evidence, but the breakdown of millions of families cannot now be gainsaid. We are beyond the possibility of liberal optimism about family life, and must reflect and reconsider. But the approach here is slightly more focused. It concentrates on marriage, and effectively ignores children and family life. There are three reasons for this. First, it is the breakdown of many marriages which seems to me to be at the core of our present crisis; if marriages are strong, then families are. Second, many sociologists see marriage as part of family life and fail to recognise its integrity as an institution in its own right. This seems worth correcting. Third, marriage *and* family are too vast a subject matter for one book. Because so few sociology books look just at marriage, there could be valuable contributions to be made to this massive issue which is central to so many people's lives.

But the book is also a different kind of sociological text. Many studies aim to be behavioural, value-free or report attitudes and meanings without an explicit perspective. For twenty or so years that approach has seemed to me epistemologically flawed and avoids many of the issues that occur in life. It has allowed sociology to be disengaged and otherworldly. Not surprisingly the discipline has undergone some decline as a result of this otherworldliness. This book adopts a perspective which accepts norms, values and views of the world to be necessary to sociology, as they are to living. This does not mean that sociology cannot be a rigorous discipline, but it cannot construct a theoretical infallibility outside values and faith. Indeed, the book goes further in espousing a Christian perspective as the necessary one for the fullest level of insight into the meaning of personhood, marriage and family. Not all readers may agree with me, but it will be clear what the roots of my thinking are. Although the Christian faith is the source of my perceptions, those insights are still muddied by the writer. Nevertheless, the sociological perspective which emerges from this approach allows a critical questioning of Western meanings and culture. It allows one to be neither modernist nor postmodernist, both institutional and subjective, both structural and action-orientated. So there is a different kind of sociology going on here, for better or worse.

The book also engages as a Christian study in a slightly different way from many others. Biblical study, theology and ethics, it could be argued, have not engaged socially for much of their recent history. Issues in family sociology are being thrown up every month, but much theology and ethics has been too *a priori* to touch them. Biblical study has also been done without social awareness, and only now is systematic thematic social study being undertaken. Such study must, for example, be cross-cultural, because the historical span of the Bible is. In this book, in order to present conclusions quickly, much of the interpretive and theological background is left implicit. They seem to me to be quite orthodox, but I hope they convey something of the riches which I find in biblical revelation waiting to be mined by further study. In addition, I find the extent to which the Scriptures interpret and judge human cultures so compelling that it puts far less emphasis on our interpretation of them. When you are on the operating table, the consultant examines you, not you her. Thus, this book aims to be Christian sociology, not theology or ethics.

This study immediately grows out of membership of the Church of England Board of Social Responsibility's Working Party on the Family. I resigned from the Working Party after demurring from some of its conclusions, but thank them for what was shared. The longer-term context is the Family Perspectives module which I have taught at Oak Hill College for about a decade. I thank all the members of those groups for what they have shared and taught me, and my colleagues, and Wendy Bell, the Oak Hill Librarian. The Ilkley Group has also frequently discussed many of these issues, and I am grateful to them for their insights. Webs of friends in Britain and overseas are tangled round its production and I thank them. And finally there is Elaine. Her sharing, counselling, thought, analysis and insight in this area are a continual part of my daily life, and they have contributed deeply to this book. The debt is huge and I gladly acknowledge it. And she is my wife as well.

1

WESTERN MARRIAGE

The universality of marriage

Marriage is universal throughout human cultures. There are variant patterns which we shall shortly discuss, but it is easy to overlook the fact that throughout human history in every culture most men and women have been married – monogamous, faithful, permanent marriage. There used to be a theory that humankind had moved from promiscuity to marriage with civilisation. Not so, said Westermarck in his magisterial study: 'It is by no means among the very lowest races that sexual relations most nearly approach to promiscuity; we find that many or most of them are completely or almost completely monogamous and that among some of them divorce is said to be unknown,' (Westermarck, 1925, I, 124–5). Overwhelmingly, men and women come to maturity and find a mate with whom they share their lives. We often focus on cultural diversity, but the universality of this institution demands attention. General Su Wu in *c.* 100 BC must leave for the wars and writes a poem to his wife,

> Since my hair was plaited and we became man and wife
> The love between us was never broken by doubt.
>
> (Waley, 1960, 39)

None of these issues is new. Tacitus notes that in Germany adultery is rare and women marry as virgins, making one lasting agreement. Children are breast-fed and not killed if economic circumstances are bad. He compares it with the corruption and vice in Roman marriage at the time (Pomeroy, 1975, 212). Whatever the place, whatever the area, marriage is crucial to the agenda of every culture.

But it also involves variations. In quite a few cultures polygamy has been found among some of the population. Men take mistresses. Often marriage is contained within highly traditional patterns of ritual. Homosexual and lesbian relationships are found in ancient and modern cultures. And ideas of what marriage means vary significantly. Sometimes it means the wife walking twenty paces behind her husband, at other times it means more or less complete submission to the mother-in-law, and on other occasions it involves being washed in goat's milk by your husband. What is going on in all these various patterns? In the rest of this chapter to help get a grip on these issues we shall identify some key cultural models which can be seen to have shaped the meaning of marriage throughout history.

Judaeo-Christian marriage

The Judaeo-Christian view of marriage has undoubtedly been world-dominant in several senses. The Jewish diaspora and Christian missionary activity spread it to the Mediterranean and Europe and to most other countries worldwide. It has been fairly basic to European attitudes to marriage, especially since the Reformation. It has also become important in Africa, South and North America and much of Asia and Australasia. The Judaeo-Christian view is thus directly spread through many cultures throughout much of recorded history. But it is also world-dominant in a second sense, in claiming to be a *universal* understanding of the meaning of marriage, and here its deeper influence lies. For it claims to define the necessary structure of marriage and to set out the norms through which it is meant to be lived. These are fairly powerful claims and they will be examined in greater depth later. Here we begin by sketching this perspective and identifying some of its key features.

The biblical Creation account records that man and woman were created by God for one another. Marriage is therefore seen as a created institution expressing in part what humankind is. The mutuality of man and woman is reflected in the union of marriage. This is defined in the great statement of Genesis 2:24. 'For this reason a man will leave his father and mother and be united to his wife, and they will become one flesh.' This statement incorporates a whole range of significant understandings – the process of moving from family dependence into the integrity of adult choice, the *monogamous* nature of marriage, the unqualified nature of the union of husband and wife and the location of sexual intercourse within the relationship of marriage. Marriage is thus seen as part of God's good created purposes for humankind. It is deeply affirmed as part of human existence and later laws like the prohibition of adultery uphold the central goodness of this relationship. It is a relationship of love and volition, not of power or family control. It is presented as the way, by choice, human beings are called to live. From this understanding of the created meaning of marriage at the beginning of Genesis Jewish and Christian thought has developed down the centuries.

Alongside this portrayal of marriage the pages of the Bible give a picture of its pathology, patterns that are wrong or misdirected, and which are identified and exposed as such. Soon polygamous marriages emerge. Lamech emerges as a figure who boasts to his wives that he has murdered a man who injured him, presumably warning them not to get any uppity ideas (Gen. 4:19–24). Later Patriarchs are polygamous, generating relationships full of jealousy and rivalry between offspring. There are marriages dominated by male violence and the treating of wives as possessions. These sinful patterns shape much of the subsequent history of the Israelites and stand alongside the witness to what marriage is, which is also elaborated in greater detail throughout the Old and New Testaments in the Mosaic Law, through the witness of couples, in poetry and prophecy. When the

Pharisees try to justify divorce, Jesus responds with a statement which stands at the centre of the Christian understanding of marriage and its pathology.

> 'Haven't you read,' he replied, 'that at the beginning the Creator "made them male and female", and said, "For this reason a man will leave his father and mother and be united to his wife, and the two will become one flesh"? So they are no longer two, but one. Therefore what God has joined together, let no one separate.'
>
> 'Why then,' they asked, 'did Moses command that a man give his wife a certificate of divorce and send her away?'
>
> Jesus replied, 'Moses permitted you to divorce your wives because your hearts were hard. But it was not this way from the beginning. I tell you that anyone who divorces his wife, except for marital unfaithfulness, and marries another woman commits adultery.'

(Matt. 19:4–9).

The weight of Jesus's insistence on the created nature of marriage and the wrongness of departing from faithfulness is overwhelmingly clear. Thus, the Judaeo-Christian view is one which identifies marriage, not as an ideal, but as an institution within which couples are called to live. At the same time it identifies destructive patterns of breakdown in human behaviour which are described in terms of adultery, lust, boasting and fault-finding. Thus it identifies what marriage is, the way it goes wrong, and fortunately, also, how relationships can be restored.

The historical outworking of this perspective is a study in itself, but there are permanent elements in it which distinguish its emphases. First, it begins with marriage, which is then seen as the *foundation* for family life. Other views see family relationships as prior and see marital relations as generated within that context. Second, from the very beginning it sees marriage as having its own integrity as a *social institution*. It is no mere pawn of state, conquest or economic forces, but stands in its own right as part of the creation order. Third, marriage is a *voluntary union* between a man and a woman involving companionship, sexual intimacy and love. It is not a matter of power and male domination. And fourth, it involves *norms* of living. Some, like faithfulness and sexual exclusivity are specific to marriage, and others like respect, gentleness and care are relevant to all relationships and especially important in the intimacy of marriage. The cultural outworking of this perspective has been long and interesting. It has involved cultural conflict with other views which have claimed Christian allegiance, but overall it has been the orthodox viewpoint and its formative power cannot be doubted. No one reading this text will have been uninfluenced by it. Later we shall examine it more fully.

Family-dominated marriage

However, there is a second great model of marriage which is of cultural importance. This sees marriage as contained within and shaped by family life. The family has been a powerful social and economic unit which has shaped a great deal of human history. The period of the Patriarchs in the Bible was largely family history. In many cultures the family has been the archetypal institution. Family dynasties have often ruled countries. In many traditional societies the heads of the family are effective rulers; the Godfather in Mafia families is just an extreme example. Many traditional African and Asian cultures fit this pattern, which has an overall religious significance. Thus, *ancestor worship* is central to many traditional cultures expressing their central commitment to the family progenitors as the source of life, wisdom and magic. The greatest sin in traditional China and Japan was lack of reverence for the father.

The model structures marriage in a number of ways. Often the family is given authority to establish the marriage of its children, and so *arranged marriages* tend to be normal. The marriage was to be the one which suited the parents; it may have involved property deals, territory or just the understanding that the partner had to fit in with the parents. The new married couple could live with her parents, a *matrilocal marriage*, or with his parents, a *patrilocal marriage*. The matrilocal marriage was one where the family retained control over the offspring of the women. It was easy for the husband to remain a guest, fathering the continuation of the family, but having little role in establishing an independent marriage and family. Sometimes he might come and go and often the maternal uncles become additional fathers to the children. Here, too, the line of descent is traced through the women; the family is *matrilineal*. This pattern is found in Africa among the Ashanti, Kongo and other tribes, among the Pueblo, Hopi and other Indian tribes and some other isolated groups, but it is not common. Generally in these cases, the family form dominates the marriage and imposes quite strong constraints on it.

The *patrilocal marriage* has been far more important, especially in Japan, China, other parts of the Far East and Africa. In Europe its strongest roots are in Roman culture. Here the marriage is located close to the father's family, and the line of succession is traced through the men – a *patrilineal* pattern. Sometimes control of the marriage was well-nigh complete; the potential marriage partners did not see one another before the wedding. Often it took place at an early age, largely on the basis of wealth, status and education. Eventually the husband grew towards the position of *pater familias*. This Roman term conveyed that the wife and children were under the power of the family head; Constantine annulled the sovereignty of the *pater familias* after his conversion to Christianity. Sometimes concubines would also fulfil the husband's needs for children or sex. Often the wife faced a mother-in-law problem because she had to submit to the authority of her husband's mother, whom she often called, 'The Great One'! There are also many sad Chinese and Japanese tales of a lonely wife dragged away from her own family by an arranged marriage who then commits suicide. Sometimes a couple in love flee from an arranged marriage which would part them (the Willow Pattern Plate myth was an English version of this theme!). Behind this model is often the sacred identity of the male Emperor as god and a pattern of ancestor worship, which will carry on as the central reality of intimate social life.

Thus, here marriage is dominated by the families of the couple. We can see how this is at odds with the biblical emphasis on leaving parents to establish a marriage. The Patriarchs, of course, moved in part into this family-dominated culture. It is interesting to see Abraham wrestling with this issue in Genesis 24. He aims to arrange a marriage for Isaac, but it is based on prayer rather than his own wishes and he does not himself choose the bride. He insists on patrilocation – 'do not take my son back there' (Gen. 24:6) – but because of the promises of God.

Family-dominated marriage, especially of a patriarchal kind, has thus shaped many cultures – ancient Rome, most of Asia, the Middle East and Africa, Hindu and Islamic views. Yet it has waned as a cultural force substantially through its contact with Christianity. Other factors helping this decline were the move from family to individual employment in industrial societies and migration. Yet we could be overstating the case. Informally, it is still present in many Western communities. The Mafia and other traditional families transferred largely intact to the West, as *West Side Story* or *The Godfather* conveyed. The 1970s' US television series, *Dallas* and *Dynasty*, were based upon a strong model of family dominance. Young and Willmott observed a matriarchal pattern in the East End of London after the Second World War. Mum, the wife's mother, is central. She finds a home for her daughter after marriage which is close by or even upstairs, and she helps bring up the children. The proverb, 'My son's a son till he gets him a wife, My daughter's a daughter all of her life' shapes the marriage (Young and Willmott, 1962, 44–74). Later we shall consider some other aspects of this great formative perspective and its influence on marriage.

Marriage and power

The two previous perspectives were normative, held in place by Jewish, Confucian or Christian moral codes. This next model runs like a dark immoral stain through history. It just affirms brute force. Some people, normally men, gain power over others and this is built into the culture of marriage and family life. Conquest, weapons, control, and domination have been widespread throughout human history. The idea of Stone Age man with a club in one hand and his wife's hair in the other is probably unfair to many Stone Age couples who were tender and caring, but it is partly true. Rape and obtaining wives by conquest have been, and sadly are, a large part of human history. Slavery has deeply shaped Greek and Roman life, much of the history of pagan Europe, the quasi-Christian conquest of South America and the history of Negroes in the United States and the West Indies. The direct evil of much of this history is beyond reporting. Kidnapping twenty million people from Africa obviously left millions of families bereaved and destroyed; we cannot guess what was done to African family and marital life by slavery. Also sinister was the way it was later rationalised. There is abundant evidence that white men and sometimes women used black slaves for sexual gratification, but the idea was that the Blacks were innately promiscuous (Jordan, 136–78). Women were treated as breeders of slaves. In Lynchburg, Virginia, a paper boasted of a slave woman aged forty-two who had had forty-one children and was now pregnant, and one church used the income from slave women to pay their pastors for sixty-eight years (Bennett, 1964, 85–6). Thus the destruction of marriage and family life caused by white colonial economic and political control is vast.

But the same has happened in class terms. It is interesting how Marx and Engels are misunderstood. In the *Communist Manifesto* they talk of the abolition of the family. How shameful! But listen:

> On what foundation is the present family, the bourgeois family, based? On capital, on private gain. In its completely developed form this family exists only among the bourgeoisie. But this state of things finds it complement in the practical absence of the family among the proletarians, and in public prostitution. Do you charge us with wanting to stop the exploitation of children by their parents? To this crime we plead guilty ... all family ties among the proletarians are torn asunder and their children transformed into simple articles of commerce and instruments of labour.

They were right. Over eighty thousand working-class prostitutes were largely servicing the well-to-do in London alone. Destructive cheap child labour was rife. Women were working as manual labourers and servants in ways which undermined family life. Housing was often squalid and working-class men were grossly overworked. So that some families could flourish, many others were destroyed. The irony of Marx and Engels was completely missed. Although this pattern has been ameliorated in the West somewhat, many couples in poor countries are struggling to enable and support Western affluence.

Men have also dominated women within marriage. This has happened physically. Wife-beating, lauded in Shakespeare's *The Taming of the Shrew*, has been common throughout history. In late nineteenth-century Liverpool one street was called 'Kicking Alley', because that was what the husbands did to their wives. There are still now in all continents, including our own, considerable problems of domestic violence. But the control has also been economic. Men have controlled the family purse. Wives have often been workers; indeed, that seems to be the dominant interpretation of African polygamy. Often women work harder than men and for men. The law has often been on the husband's side, and marriage has therefore been definitively shaped by the motive of male control. Women have assumed it is normal. Thus the structure of marriage in many cultures has had *patriarchy*, or male power, built into it. The pattern of patriarchy has not been as complete as some radical feminists would avow, but it is deeply influential.

Again, Christianity stands deeply opposed to this. The way Jesus consistently opposed all expressions of dominant power and 'turned the other cheek' marks the greatest defeat of power in human history. Paul describes Jesus as 'nailing the principalities and powers to the cross'; this instrument of human intimidation carries intimidating power after the resurrection. The gentle power of the Holy Spirit is the power to serve others, not dominate them. And this influences marriage. The old Church of England wedding service where the husband promises, 'with all my worldly good, I thee endow' conveys the different flavour. This is not power, but willing sharing and tenderness as the basis of the relationship. Sadly, Christians have repeatedly compromised these truths, and throughout history there has been a war as to whether peaceful and uncoercive attitudes should shape marriage or those that express colonial, class and male domination.

Romantic marriage

The previous models are quite easily recognisable. Marriage is union, locked in the family, or male-dominated. The next model is slightly more difficult to see objectively, because it was based on a fundamental cultural change which was religious in nature. It involved a move from a Christian world view to one which was Human-centred, a move from worshipping God to worshipping Man as the central focus of existence. In the eighteenth-century Enlightenment, especially among the landed gentry, Christian reverence for God was pushed into the background and, instead, a religious belief in humankind became central. For those who converted, this was a fundamental revolution in thought and attitude which also deeply changed the dynamics and understanding of marriage. Man and/or woman became objects of worship. According to this view marriage is not an institution which man and women enter on God-given terms, but it is a relationship which *people themselves create*. They are the arbiters of the way they should live. But the change is not only in the view of the relationship, but in the self-understanding of men and women, for man and woman become objects of worship. In Christian theology God is the Creator of gender, man and woman, and is not gendered by nature. Men and women are created for one another. But here man and woman become gods. Venus, the goddess of beauty, became a female idiom of power and fatal attraction. The Man, as Philosopher–King, Warrior, Hero, Sportsman and Superman emerged as a similar deity. Thus, *man worship* and *woman worship* became part of the culture, and this was reflected in the emergence of *romantic love* as the defining characteristic of the relationship between them. There is much discussion about the weight of romantic love in different cultures, but most conclude that as a major social force it only emerged at the end of the eighteenth century with the Romantic movement (Shorter, 1975; Praz, 1970; Pearsall, 1971; De Rougemont, 1983; Storkey, 1994, ch. 3). Here love was an all-consuming relationship which expressed the meaning of life. These changes were massive. Persons made marriage. The human, male or female, was the ultimate reality and love was basically sexual passion.

The people who formed and disseminated these views thought they were encouraging human progress, but actually through the Grand Tour of Europe by the aristocratic élites, they were drawing on old European pagan religions. These had gendered deities. The most obvious are the Greek gods and goddesses, Zeus, Apollo, Hermes, Athena, Hesta and Hecate, which gave a gendered deification of war, childbearing or witchcraft. Linked to this was an idealisation of the male and (later) the female form, which we recognise from Greek and Hellenistic sculpture, the Olympics and other games. The outcome of this pattern was first a culture of male adulation with women seen largely as child factories, but also strong female idolatry, especially later. This Greek pattern is reflected in many other cultures. The Yin-Yang (Chinese) or In-Yo (Japanese) philosophies see basic male and female principles as reflected throughout the universe. The whole of reality is thus interpreted in gendered terms. With the Renaissance and Enlightenment these patterns were reintroduced to European art, culture, courting and marriage. No longer were the deities gendered, but gender was deified.

Man worship has become a strong part of European culture. Because many men claim to live in a secular culture, they would reject this description, but it is no less. In the Renaissance it was expressed in the idiom of the *Universal Man*, '*l'uomo universale*', accomplished in everything. The belief in the complete man was overwhelming. Apollo, Bacchus, Hercules, Mercury, Brutus and other classical figures were drafted in to create the image. The great politician and artist became a central figure in this idiom. Lorenzo il Magnifico, Leonardo and Michelangelo were expressing the glory of man. Leon Battista Alberti could say, 'Men can do all things if they will.' Man is the measure of all things. He strives for the perfect soul. He is self-made (Burckhardt, 1965, 81–103). This centrality of Man changes relationships between men and women. Here first, in De Beauvoir's famous words, 'He is the Subject, he is the Absolute – she is the Other' (1972, 16). In the eighteenth-century the male self idiom changes to the rational man, and subsequently the passionate, the strong, the poetic, the controlling, the business and the action man become the male focus of self-veneration. These processes of self-worship are so strong in the formation of culture, especially since the formation of film, that they will contribute to much of our later analysis.

There was also a female form. It often had a subtle form; woman was the inspiration for man – Beatrice for Dante, Laura for Petrarch. Some women were *Viragos*, that is, women who were the equal of men in accomplishments and sensitivity. But this kind of relationship took place outside marriage. Others offered inspiration by beauty and sex, perhaps as courtesans – they were *Venuses* to be worshipped. A third model was based on the Virgin Mary, offering a model of the pure woman who could be worshipped as the central meaning of family life, the *Madonna* figure. The impact of this view waned somewhat with the Reformation, Counter-Reformation and later Christian revivals, although idealisations of women flourished in poetry, art and opera in the nineteenth century. With the twentieth century and Hollywood woman-worship became a cultural flood, moving through from the pretty consort to the *sex goddess*. Romantic love was cast as a relationship between the god and the goddess, the hero and the heroine. They have been through many permutations, but the underlying faith is clear. Or rather, it is not clear, because it is so much part of the dogma of our age that we cannot see it any more.

This model sets up a different view of marriage. It depends on a human-centred view of reality and is not contained within an institutional structure. The Judaeo-Christian emphasis on mutuality is lost in favour of two poles of worship: Man and Woman are gods and goddesses constructing their own relationships, and the central meaning of love is rooted in human passion rather than in God's creation of the universe. The outworking of this cultural vision we shall consider more fully in the next chapter.

The Moral Shell

This next model is the corruption of the Christian one, and it has been widely experienced by those who have not accepted the Christian faith, but have lived in a culture which still contains many of its formal characteristics. For Christianity involves an awareness of a God-given identity, of living in an open and central relationship with God, and of being obedient to the laws of God and the teachings of Christ. Love and faithfulness derive their meaning from Christian revelation and the character of God. Christianity affirms that you cannot distance yourself from the God in whom you live and move and have your being. In other words, it has to affect the totality of life. However, those who have not accepted this faith have tended to develop an approach to life which has a different focus. They have looked on faith from outside and have understood the meaning of marriage in *moralistic terms*. The result has tended to be a formal, rule-orientated response to life and to marriage. Many have been prepared to have a Christian wedding but reject the idea that Christianity might influence their marriage thereafter. This perspective emphasises that extra-marital sex, adultery and divorce are wrong, but does not address the meaning and motivations shaping love and marriage. The actual interpretation of many supposed Victorian moral attitudes is now being questioned, for it is clear that often they have been interpreted in self-validating liberal ways. Far from being oppressive, moral reform was often the means of liberating people from oppressive personal lives (Himmelfarb, 1995). Gradually, however, the moralistic view came to be seen as oppressive in a variety of ways – the prohibition of premarital sex, faithfulness in marriage, staying with a relationship for life – all of these have seemed to be increasingly irksome, because another central motivation is working within them. But nevertheless the weight of the moral code has been very strong. Many have appealed to it as a basic social cement and as what gives society order, and it has stuck as an external coercive force for a long while.

The question is, what has given this moral code its weight and authority, when it is no longer based on a response to God and a Christian understanding of the nature of human relationships? There are a number of possible contenders. One is the *Law*. The State decrees certain behaviour and excludes others, and for many it therefore defines what should be regarded as morally correct or incorrect behaviour. Another is *Society*, or social groups and peer pressure. The question of what other people might regard as right or wrong and the extent to which they exert pressure to conformity. In rural Wales, for example, when a middle-aged widow was being visited at night by a young lad the local youth groups stuffed up the chimney and threw vermin in the house (Frankenberg, 62). A shotgun marriage, where the man who made the girl pregnant was required, down the barrel of a gun, to marry her, had a similar effect. Another is the *Church*, seen as a moral institution. But we seem to have moved from communities operating with strong social norms to ones which are more anonymous and *laissez-faire*. Gradually, this pressure has eased. The underlying model which has grown out of this view is often quite Freudian. People are a seething mass of desires, sexual and personal, which often drive them to certain ways of behaving, but these are controlled, or suppressed, by moral and legal codes which help to maintain the fabric of society. The individual was therefore seen as a warring ground between the instinctual 'id' and the suppressing moral 'superego'. But in the late twentieth century the *individual* has come to be seen as the central concept around which moral codes should be shaped. Rights, happiness, freedom and self-fulfilment have changed the content of previous codes and emptied the idea of morality, ungrounded in Christian revelation, of any substantial content.

Thus, *moralism*, often associated with Victorian values in

England, or the 'Moral Majority' in the States has often become hollow in the experience of modern Western couples, but its impact remains great. The fact that Jesus, Paul and orthodox Christianity have all strongly critiqued an external moral code and adherence to rules has often been ignored as people seek some basis for secure relationships.

Individualism and contract

The other great modern Western model of marriage is individualist in its focus. Gradually, as a person withdraws from a relationship with God and loses the meaning of neighbour relationships, the central point of reference for life is often sought in the self. Life then happens in relation to the individual. This focus has been present in European culture since the Enlightenment, although in the early twentieth century it was obscured by the great collectivisms of class, nation and race. But slowly it has emerged. Individual happiness became a focus for relationships. Sex as self-gratification became emphasised. Individual rights were asserted. Choice became an unqualified good; one could not make a wrong or bad choice. How tenuous this view was as a basis for living has been evident to commentators for a long time. Veblen sent it up at the beginning of the century.

The hedonistic calculator of man is that of a lightning calculator of pleasures and pains, who oscillates like a homogeneous globule of desire of happiness under the impulse of stimuli which shift him about the area, but leave him intact. He has neither antecedent nor consequence. He is an isolated, definitive human datum in stable equilibrium except for the buffets of the impinging forces that displace him in one direction or another. Self-imposed in elemental space, he spins symmetrically about his own spiritual axis until the parallelogram of forces bears down upon him, whereupon he follows the line of the resultant. When the force is spent, he comes to rest, a self-contained globule of desire as before.

(Veblen, 1969, 73–4).

But often ideas flourish, not because they are right, but because they have powerful backers, and this approach was pushed by the sellers, the advertisers, the media audience grabbers and the capitalists. Money was invested in this view. Having a hamburger became a way of life and a defining view of relationships. If this one doesn't suit, then I drive a little further and get another. The standards of interpersonal behaviour grow from within the individual. What is good for me, is valid behaviour. Now this viewpoint, stupid though it is, is a cultural steamroller with millions invested in it, clanking through history unchecked.

This model claims to change the inner meaning of marital and quasi-marital relationships. The Christian idea of a union is from this perspective not valid, for each partner must define a relationship on their own terms and not as subject to some common norms. Thus, the relationship becomes contractual, a matter of negotiation between the partners. In a subtle way it becomes external to the individual identity of each partner and not a union which defines who they are from henceforth. Gradually, a proportion of modern relationships has come to reflect this character. Cohabitation has emerged as a relational model which allows a more limited expression of partnership. Many view marriage as not necessarily permanent. The impact of this view has been to create a great sea change in the character of marriage in the West, and through the West to the rest of the world. Again, we shall look much more thoroughly at this perspective in the next chapter.

Knowing what marriage is

This chapter has presented six great models of marriage which are in cultural competition with one another. Some sociologists used to believe that we could consider views of marriage and other relationships neutrally and without values. I deem this to be impossible epistemologically, and an approach which impoverishes analysis (Storkey, 1993). It also begs a range of questions about our human condition. Most sociologists in this area have actually adopted a family-centred perspective. Westermarck, Malinowski, Goode and Fletcher and structural-functionalists have all done so. Fletcher's summary is 'that the family is not rooted in marriage, but marriage is an institution rooted in the family' (Fletcher, 1966, 22). Feminist writers have rightly revealed the significance of male power. Fewer sociologists have considered critically the individualist, romantic and moralist perspectives, partly because sociologists have tended to be part of a benign liberal culture. This study will do that. It is shaped by Christian understanding, and, because a Christian perspective on marriage often remains unexplored in sociology and culture, it deliberately explores Christian views.

In my judgement, family-centred marriage has some, but limited, significance in the West. Male power has been exposed by feminist and other writers, although it is still doing much damage. But the rampant models are the individualist, romantic and moralist. They are generating a level of crisis in Western marital relationships which is neither understood nor addressed by the way we live. In the next chapter we confront this more immediate situation.

2

MARRIAGE IN CRISIS?

Dogma and social thought

One of the problems of any culture is that it finds great difficulty in getting outside itself. As the baboon said to his friend, 'Look, his bum is white!' Over many decades the dominant culture in the West has been a variety of forms of humanism, like individualism and romanticism. This liberal culture has assumed that it is presiding over a pattern of human progress which is automatically for the better, and it has espoused a particular perspective on marriage without questioning its deepest roots. That perspective impels cultural development in a certain direction. Thus, restricting divorce would curtail individual freedom. We should be free to establish our own forms of sexual relationship. Consumer culture is good for family life. Romantic love cannot be gainsaid. Actually, of course, there has been a complex mixing of marital cultures, but over the last few decades this liberal individualism has had a remarkable dominance. Partly, this is because it has had a strong alliance with business and finance and has pushed a consumerist culture. The members of this liberal élite have been advocating freedom, which has also meant *their* freedom to be big earners, big spenders and free in sexual relationships. Such a dominant culture tends to produce dogma, unchallenged thoughts and ways of seeing things, and this has happened in the West. Often churches have espoused the same liberalism in their theology. In education the liberal dogma that progress will happen has undermined the critical faculties of many scholars. In sociology it is very interesting that although the evidence for the problems created by divorce has been strong for many decades, it has been viewed benignly. Typical is this American text: 'Contributing to greater freedom in the marital relationship is the freedom to get out of it. Divorce has become a viable, fairly acceptable alternative ... Psychology's nonmoralistic, nonblaming views of people, marriage, and divorce gradually encouraged people to accept the reality of marital problems ... Marriage has come a long way – from a closed, restricted and restricting relationship' (McGinnis and Finnegan, 1976, 21). For decades this liberal individualist view of relationships has been dominant and relatively unquestioned.

But now things have changed. We have around us so much evidence of the problems which it has created that it cannot be ignored. Whereas in the 1960s and 1970s adultery provided the happy ending, now films and soaps must consider its consequences. Great media marriages explode across our consciousness in bright colour and then fizzle into divorce. Richard Burton and Elizabeth Taylor, Woody Allen and Mia Farrow, Charles and Diana have all exposed the pain and failure of divorce. And as I write, the West trial has just examined the murders of ten young women by a sexually obsessed couple. Sexual liberation is not quite so great as it was, but we know it too in our own lives. We all are, or know, people who have gone through divorce. Children in vast numbers have effectively lost a parent. No one involved in counselling and therapy would deny the seriousness of the trends which were previously viewed so benignly. Now we have to question the received orthodoxy of liberal optimism. In this chapter we look at some of the weaknesses which are now exposed.

Is marriage in crisis?

The straightforward answer to this question is to look at levels of divorce. It is actually quite difficult to establish what proportion of marriages end in this way. A cohort needs to be followed through for twenty or more years to see what proportion end in divorce and this cannot easily be done and figures for divorce rates are often not as informative as they sometimes claim to be. Divorce rates often overstate the rates for cohorts, and more recently they have become more opaque because cohabitation has obscured further relationships which break down. Nevertheless, the big picture is not difficult to establish. Marriage relationships began to fail first in Russia after the Revolution. Divorce could be registered by either spouse without assigning reasons until 1944. Levels stayed high, especially affected by drink and inadequate housing, and after the Second World War the other countries of Eastern Europe, especially Czechoslovakia, began to experience a similar trend. In the United States there has also been a high level of divorce going back to the beginning of the century. By the end of the Second World War the figure had climbed to nearly half a million and it rose to over a million in the early 1980s (Riley, 1991). Germany and France, which had had relatively high rates early in the century stabilised, but other countries took off. Initially the lead was taken by Scandinavia, especially Sweden, which broke through to really high levels in the 1970s. Britain started more slowly, but the levels of marital breakdown were among the highest by the 1980s. The Catholic countries of southern Europe showed the lowest levels of divorce, partly because their laws were tighter, and even in the middle European Catholic countries like Poland and Belgium levels are noticeably lower.

The overall situation now is that the highest levels of divorce are found in the United States and Russia with about half of first marriages ending in divorce. In Britain, Sweden and Denmark the figure is, say, four in ten, in mid-Europe around a quarter, slightly higher in Eastern Europe, and in the Southern Catholic countries fewer than one in ten end in divorce. It is clear, therefore, that there has been a substantial tide of divorce, year after year, which does not look like ebbing and is bringing with it a second wave of cohabitation, which signals a scaling down of formal marriage commitment. How do we interpret these changes?

First, the trend of marital breakdown is clear and unabated. It is something like a threefold increase in thirty years in Europe. It is unprecedented in modern Western history and even in world history. This suggests that there are wider cultural and social changes involved, rather than answers like X and Y happened to marry the wrong persons. Second, there are substantial variations between countries and it can be said that these reflect in part the stringency of divorce laws in Catholic countries, but the social outcome is possibly different for religious reasons, and we might need to take account of this. Few commentators yet congratulate the Catholic Church for the extent to which it has kept marriages together in Southern Europe. However, another level of question is how marital breakdown is to be interpreted, and this is quite complex. For example, many feel that a marriage ending in divorce calls into question the whole basis of the relationship. Others may say that it was good for a while. Again, as we have seen, divorce is often viewed benignly as part of the individual freedom of the modern age. Yet these views are often unrealistic. To leave a person to whom one has been so intimately committed is a level of rejection which goes beyond most human experience. Seldom does it not involve heartache, hurt and grief for at least one partner which is fairly overwhelming. These figures therefore represent a scale of personal tragedy which adds up to one of the greatest crises we have faced socially in the West. It is a crisis of marriage.

Has marriage failed?

Hitherto the answer has often been that marriage has failed. When a relationship enters difficulty or breaks down, it is *the marriage* which is to blame, and the individuals should

be able to get out of the marriage and start new relationships. With this approach, there is nothing wrong with
ending a relationship, as long as it is right for the individual
concerned. *No-fault divorce* has come to be seen as the
principle for divorce reform. Many have claimed that there
is overwhelming evidence for the failure of marriage and
look for some other kind of progressive relationship. The
trend began with Edmund Leach's *Reith Lectures* in 1967.
The most famous statement was, 'Far from being the basis
of the good society, the family, with its narrow privacy and
tawdry secrets, is the source of all our discontents,' (Reith,
693). It continued with David Cooper's *The Death of the
Family*, and Laing and Esterson's studies (1970) of the way
some families generated schizophrenia (Fletcher, 1988).
More recently, Hafner has given an account of why 'monogamy isn't working' in a book entitled *The End of Marriage*.
The weight of these views needs to be sifted carefully. They
identify the fact that some children have a bad time and
some marriages end. But perhaps half of children and
couples probably do have substantially good relationships,
and some of this writing is therefore overstating the case.
These books tend to examine the pathological end of the
spectrum and they also open up some of the destructive
internal dynamics of family life, which we shall examine
later. But more to the point is the kind of special pleading
which comes from this way of seeing things. *Marriage* is the
problem, because *a priori I* cannot be. Because the individual is sovereign and can in the deepest sense do no wrong,
when problems occur in the relationship, they must be
externalised on the marriage. So we talk of the breakdown
of marriage and, indeed, think of some kind of fatalistic
process whereby this outcome had to be. This fatalism is
repeated regularly in sociological studies and the media.

But, of course, there is another answer. Once the individual is prepared to call into question their own character and
approach to the marriage, it is possible that the problem
does not lie with marriage as an institution, but with the

attitudes and behaviour of one or more of the partners in the marriage. This, of course, is the Christian approach. 'If we say that we have no sin, we deceive ourselves, and the truth is not in us. If we acknowledge our sins, God is faithful and just, to forgive us our sins and to cleanse us from all unrighteousness' (1 John 1:8). And this too is sociologically and personally accurate, because we know a great number of the things that cause marital 'breakdown'. Adultery, violence, drink, quarrelling, lust, disrespect, unkindness, pride, overwork, lack of self-control and selfishness would rank high in many people's lists. Many divorcees, and married people, have a very sharp list of what is wrong with their partner. Thus, we have to ask whether the fatalistic answer of 'irretrievable breakdown', or 'no-fault divorce', posited on the understanding that really the individual is OK, gets to the bottom of the issue. The institution of marriage might be good and trustworthy, provided we are prepared to question and critique many of the individual attitudes which our culture gives us. This might be the route from *self*-deception.

But even this is not all of the picture. Many enter marriage with unquestioned commitment, and find that it falls apart in their hands. They would accept fault, if they could clearly identify it. There seems no other conclusion than that marriage *has* failed. But then the question is, What kind of marriage? And here the answer is the complex modern idioms which define marriage and marriage-like relationships in the modern West. These include individualism, moralism, romantic love and a number of other views and attitudes. The suggestion in this chapter is that when marriage has failed, it is largely marriage seen in these terms, and not marriage seen in Christian terms, which is increasingly untried.

Trends undermining marriage

In this section we shall consider a number of trends which are rooted in individualist, romantic and moralistic ways of seeing things. These go a considerable way to explaining why so many marriages have broken down and also identify the choices which have been made in our culture which help make this such a widespread trend. Although the process is complex and the weighting of these factors (and other potential ones) is difficult, we are looking at an entirely understandable trend, for which we corporately are responsible. Our question is what we do with these corporate responsibilities.

1. Lost time for marriage

Labour-saving devices and smaller families should leave more time in the home. Actually domestic life has tended to become more complicated; we use coffee machines instead of spoons, and looking after children has become more elaborate. The big change is television and video which now claims twenty hours a week viewing (ST, 1995, 216). In the United States in midwinter viewing figures used to be five hours a day. This time is taken out of relationships, especially marriage, and it contributes to the dominant feeling that many people have of being rushed. What suffers is the quality of marital sharing. One American study suggested that couples spent eleven minutes a week talking to one another. It must be more than that, but the power of television as a *retreat* from relationships in the home must be great, and its impact on marital sharing devastating. Television grows from and promotes a culture of individual gratification.

2. Marriage as leisure

There is a strong emphasis in modern culture on work and leisure. Work is costly and demanding, and leisure is reward. They give at work and receive at home. Within this perspective home and marriage are seen as reward. What couples are taught to expect is that their partners will give them rewards in terms of company, sex, comfort and lifestyle. But, of course, this model will not work, because both cannot receive at home; there must be give and take, and the business of marriage needs a lot of work. The traditional model was of the wife giving and the husband receiving when he came home. This has now substantially broken down with nothing to take its place except the priorities of the wants of individuals.

3. Pre-marital sexual partners

About 20 per cent of young men aged 25–34 in Britain have no or one sexual partner, but nearly 55 per cent have had five or more (Wellings, 95). So more than half of the young male British population have had a sexual relationship with at least four other women than their wife. For about 30 per cent the figure is ten other women. We have to ask what this means for people's experience. Broadly, a high proportion of people have a series of premarital sexual relationships which lead through to marriage. Many are effectively practising *serial monogamy* before marriage, and it is not surprising that they do so after, either as adultery or by directly passing on to another relationship. What is lost here is the sense of the uniqueness and sanctity of marriage, where this other person alone gives and is given undivided love. The experience of being used as an early sexual partner, or of having sex without commitment, may be a lot more destructive than a liberal culture allows.

4. The meanings of love

Biblical love is rigorously defined in terms of the way we are meant to live. It is patient, kind, gentle, and forgives grievances. It is not proud, self-seeking, easily angered, rude or holding on to a record of wrongs. It doesn't fail and always perseveres and is central in our relationship with God. But this kind of love has not had much cultural exposure and is probably in decline. If so, it is the most serious trend in our society. The kinds of love which people have presented to them and on the whole accept are very different. They are premised on the views of romantic love which limit love to the chemistry which occurs in a man–woman relationship. They include love as feeling, a need for happiness, an ideal or a duty. Often it is seen as sexually passionate. Being 'in love' is often subjective, experiential, sexual and unstable. All of this is conveyed exactly in the Princess Diana's *Panorama* interview. 'Yes, I adored him. Yes, I was in love with him. But I was very let down' (BBC, 20/11/95). Many now are *post-romantic*. Love is just being compatible, something you hope to achieve, putting together a lifestyle or using sexual power (Storkey, 1994). Clearly, the breakdown of the meaning of love in marriage relationships is a serious cultural issue.

5. Individualism

The individualism in our culture has had a direct impact on the meaning of marriage. A marriage union is the construction of a 'we' relationship, where identity is shared. A couple is in tune and learns to think, feel and act corporately. An individualist and subjective culture asks us to think and feel from our egos outwards, and marriage and the marriage partner become external. Daily soap operas, magazines, television and newspapers assume that one thinks in these terms. The personal processes through which this takes root in people's lives and relationships are often quite complex –

daydreaming, resentment, self-pity, want generation, desires, feeling misunderstood, fantasy, creating private areas of life and withdrawal, but the effect is to change a relationship from one which involves bonding and togetherness into one where individuals feel lonely and self-focused. Thus, we face the possibility that even within marriage and other intimate relationships, people subjectively experience themselves as lonely individuals on a scale which is vast.

6. A contract for now

This individualism has also changed the dynamics of faithfulness. Gradually the focus is changing. Instead of a commitment before God to the other person for life, for better, for worse, for richer, for poorer, the idiom is now more in terms of individual trading. The question is more 'What is in this relationship for me now?', 'Let's see how long this relationship lasts', 'If you can't give me what I want, then I'll have to look somewhere else.' The bonding of a marriage union gives way to the negotiation of a marriage relationship, or of cohabitation, which is often a more advanced form of this idiom. This change has an impact on problem thresholds. One of the issues of marriage is the question of how much I will suffer for this person. Suffering is a part of life and most couples are called at one stage or another to suffer for (not just suffer) their partner. This individualism invites a partner to cut out, to shop elsewhere.

7. The resources for marriage

In Britain over the last two decades or so there has been a growing inequality between rich and poor, largely through Conservative favouritism to the rich. It has been reflected in unemployment, poor housing and economic stagnation. In the United States and Britain for a longer period Black populations have had restricted effective access to education, training and jobs. The result has been a growing breakdown of marriage and family life which has itself added to the problem of poverty. In these situations the men, with no economic resources, have been marginalised, and the family has centred around the mother and children with unstable cohabiting and marriage relationships. Drugs, violence, alcohol and crime have often made it even more difficult for these groups. In Black groups in London 18 per cent of households were single parent with dependent children compared with 4 per cent for other groups (1991 Census). In South Wales and other areas similar patterns are found. Thus, considerable groups of the population do not have the resources or the experience to put together effective married and family life.

8. *Overwork in paid employment*

The emphasis on high rates of income as the basis for personal gratification has had another outcome. Employers in Britain, unconstrained by the European Union's Social Chapter, have been continually trading up higher levels of work for higher pay. Lower top rate income tax has also put a higher premium on being well paid. This, together with the concentration of resources in a proportion of the working population, has tended to lead to the concentration of work among some of the population. Some 35 per cent are working forty-five hours a week or more. Often they tend to be married to one another. The prior demands of jobs are very high. The energy commitment demanded, especially of the young, is considerable. Frequently, in order to boost profits, companies have laid off workers and just demanded that other employees work harder. The result has been patterns of work stress and work priority which have hurt marriage and family relationships deeply among some groups.

9. Relativised morality

In sexual and marital life a number of moral norms have
been part of British life for centuries. The biblical prohibition on adultery is one. The understanding that premarital
sex is wrong is another. Many people, a large majority in the
case of the second, have found ways of convincing themselves that these are wrong. The process is an interesting
one. Often, it is assumed that earlier generations are stupid
or naive, or that repression was the universal lot of our
forefathers and mothers. The great hinge around which
morality has swung has been the individual, because the
judge of moral codes has become *what seems good for me*.
The key assumption in magazines, films and popular ethics
is ego evaluation. 'Good' is defined by and for the subject.
The result has been the ability of groups and individuals to
override situations where harm is done to others and to
construct patterns of justification for them. 'Wider sexual
experience is a good thing (for me).' 'Our marriage relationship was a bit dead.' 'I thought I was in love.' This change is
largely media-generated and has little to do with ethical
debate. It is a tide which is still flowing strong despite its
obvious weaknesses.

10. Sex as an industry

There are now a number of industries which depend heavily
on sex, most obviously the media. Here, sex is a product
which is advertised and sold through normal marketing
techniques. A fifth or more of a nation's magazine content
may have a pornographic motive. In newspapers sexual
material is pushed, presumably because it sells, although the
commentary may be moralistic and negative. Page 3 is tit tit,
and page 4 tut tut. The produce succeeds by inducing
obsessive and addictive behaviour, like coffee and cigarettes.
With pornography the obsessions tend to be cruel and
inhuman. Fantasy is encouraged. The result is often to

induce men especially to view sex in terms of subjective arousal and gratification, and to divorce it from love. The result, presumably, is a lot of relationships where women feel used and where sex is dehumanising.

11. Isolated social units

The pressures of a consumer society generate another change. Moving job and house leaves young married couples with fewer natural contacts with friends and peers. Family breakdown often leaves relationships across the generations problematic. Smaller families reduce the numbers of brothers and sisters, uncles and aunts with which couples can relate. Age cohorts are also more isolated from one another than they used to be. When the effects of commuting distances, the impact of television and the relative physical isolation of housing units are added, it is quite clear that many households are more isolated than used to be the case. The contraction of the numbers of housewives has also weakened community networks which often used to incorporate the women of an area. As a result, many of the ways in which families and marriages learned from their elders have fallen into abeyance.

12. Gender manipulation and hostility

Relationships between the sexes have often been problematic, but in some ways they are now quite acute. Power relationships of men over women have been tackled in some areas, but still male predatory attitudes have generated high levels of mistrust among women. Many women have struggled at work with male power, sexual harassment and lack of respect for their family commitments. Many men face unemployment and loss of economic power. Marital breakdown has left many bitter relationships. Male violence in intimate relationships is common. Women use, and men agree to be used by, their sexuality for financial gain.

Against this background it is often difficult for relationships of husband–wife trust to grow and flourish.

13. The ideal home

An incredible amount of time and money has been invested in homes in the late twentieth century. They should be the scenario for ideal marriage and family life, full of warmth, fun and comfort, but in relationship terms it has often not worked out that way. The costs of funding these homes have often been great. The complexity of furnishing and running these units has often absorbed time and energy, and the activities within them have often been relationship-negating rather than enriching. Others have faced homes which are debilitating in terms of repair, costs and debt. Because homes are seen as more significant, they have been the focus of more relationship stress.

14. The second wave

We are now in a situation where many people coming to the age of marriage have experienced the break-up of the parental marriage. They therefore face the construction of a relationship in which they have no confidence and little positive experience. They are in the position of having to unlearn attitudes from their parents, rather than carry them through to their own marriages. Deeper still is the direct pain, rejection and trauma which many children of divorced parents feel. They have problems to sort out which often preclude a good stable relationship. Evidence suggests that marital breakdown can become a permanent intergenerational pattern which leaves men emotionally unable to create stable marriages and families.

15. The fragmenting ego

A number of postmodern perspectives have signalled the way in which the sense of personhood has fragmented for many people. They are asked to call into question their gender, values, morality, image, career and relationships on a scale which has seldom occurred previously. *Who the subject is* can become a quest which will be answered almost in terms of self-creation: I am whomever I make myself. Because relationships are often without overlap, there is also a sense that they have no coherence, except for the experiencing ego. Behind these experiences lies the fact that most people rarely define their lives in relation to God and a systematic body of Christian self-knowledge, but construct their own faith, often in dichotomous ways. In many marriages, at many different levels, people are trying to 'find themselves' in ways which generate problems for their relationships.

Reconstituting marriage

These summary reasons could be seen as explaining much of the pattern of marital breakdown which has been observed in Britain and throughout the West. Of course, they need much more thorough development, which will occur later in the book, but the kind of explanation on offer needs briefly to be considered. First, there are many marriages which these factors do not swamp, which work well. Second, there is nothing inevitable about these processes. Many of them depend on our attitudes, assent, commitments and priorities. Others could be addressed by reform. Third, the failure is of *these kinds of marriage*, not of marriage as understood in Christian terms. Broadly, the picture is of failure in modern liberal idioms of marriage, sex and society which could be corrected. The trend is not inevitable.

But nor is the idea of reversing the trend, or the swing

of the pendulum, for what came earlier is sometimes just as problematic. The question is what kind of marriage we should have and what kind of person we should be in our intimate relationships. Much of the current debate, including some of that generated by traditionalists in relation to the *Something to Celebrate* Report, understates the depth of the problem. For we should be calling into question not just the current trends which have helped generate this pattern of crisis, but also much of the past. We are addressing, even if by default, the way we have behaved and seen ourselves. We are probing the world view of the modern liberal West. But to do that we need a firm foundation from which to build, and to that we now turn.

3

A CHRISTIAN UNDERSTANDING
OF MARRIAGE

Introduction

This chapter is a more systematic exploration of the Christian view of marriage outlined in Chapter 1. It details a perspective which has been culturally formative, yet which is in retreat before the liberal and individualist perspective outlined in the previous chapter. Clearly, the perspective on marriage is only a part of the Christian faith, and one of the limitations of this presentation is that it must take for granted much teaching on the nature of God, biblical revelation, the doctrine of personhood and society, sin, the person of Jesus Christ, the Holy Spirit and human salvation. At the same time it tries to make explicit the way in which some of these central Christian teachings orientate us towards understanding marriage. With this in mind let us consider its structure more closely.

At one level the nature of marriage is perfectly clear and most people understand it immediately: *Marriage is the union of a man and woman for life.* Although this is the straightforward summary of this chapter, understanding what it means is more complex. For example, a human-centred view of marriage tries to construct its meaning by looking at the common characteristics of existing marriages. Many marriages do not last for life, and therefore, it could be argued, we should change the meaning of marriage to take account of this. We could say that marriage is the union of a man and a woman *for as long as it works*. There could be other similar redefinitions. But here the question of the approach to understanding marriage becomes crucial. If we begin from the failures and distorted understandings built into many human relationships and try to construct our understanding on that basis, the result is likely to be confused and contradictory. Many sociological studies of marriage try to follow that route and contain much valuable material, but still the underlying approach obscures important truths. Collecting data and examining behaviour do not uncover the insights which are necessary to know what is good for us. A Christian understanding is different. Like a doctor examining pathology, it does it from the perspective of health. It diagnoses what is wrong in relationships in terms of a God-given understanding of healthy relationships.

This means that we have a task in approaching marriage. We look at what marriage is meant to be. We try not to be caught up in the myriad of misunderstandings which are around. There is discernment, insight and self-awareness which can be had, and conversely we need an awareness of the ways in which human relationships mess up. We look at the created structure of marriage, and the ways in which it is distorted. The rest of this chapter tries to do this in a systematic way, and it is really the core of the study.

Marriage reflects and speaks to the created purpose of humankind as man and woman

First, marriage is to be understood as part of the creation; it is built into our existence. The definitive description occurs within the great Creation account of Genesis 1 and 2. God has created the whole universe by his Word of power, and this includes humankind, male and female, whose relationship is in part structured by the institution of marriage. The creation of man and woman is *very good*, part of the glory of creation and entirely affirmed. Moreover, the Creation account fixes a basic lesson for humanity which is often forgotten. 'The Lord God said, "It is *not good* for the man to be alone. I will make a helper suitable for him,"' (Gen. 2: 18). Here the goodness of the man–woman relationship is directly affirmed by God. The word, 'helper' is used frequently in Genesis of the Lord God and underlines the weight of this deliberate *mutuality*. God brings the Woman to the Man and the Man affirms, 'This is now bone of my bone and flesh of my flesh' (Gen. 2:23). Thus we see a manifold truth. The man–woman union is part of the purposes of God. Man and woman are created for one another, physiologically and personally. The man acknowledges a common identity with the woman. Marriage is instituted as part of *human* life. When Jesus was asked a question about divorce, he responded with this creation principle. 'Haven't you read,' he replied, 'that at the beginning the Creator "made them male and female"? . . .' (Matt. 19:4). Further, this is an understanding of what we *are*, not an ideal. Some classical Greek thought encourages people to think of marriage as an ideal, but, as Adam acknowledged, it is what we are – made for companionship.

We are called to live in marriage on God's terms, not to believe we can create our own

Sometimes in Western culture people think in terms of constructing their own relationships. This approach contrasts with the biblical understanding that the basic terms of our relationships are God-given, because this is the way God has made us to live. Human beings are creatures – finite, with limited understanding, deeply fallible and with given conditions of existence. The terms of life, *for our good*, are given by God. Thus, marriage is instituted for us and reflects the way we are meant to live. Essentially, this is a responsive process. It requires a sense of respect for the Creator and the humility to learn. We *enter* marriage, and we *learn* what it involves in terms of love, respect and honour of this other person. Marriage is a matter of fundamental obedience to God and God's commandments, because there is no other way to live in marriage. This principle operates at many different levels. Adultery is forbidden, because it dishonours and hurts the partner. Love must be patient. It is bad to let the sun go down on your anger, and we are therefore called to submit our anger to God's precepts. The humility of being a creature before God is therefore crucial to life and to learning about marriage. It puts us in our place and allows us to see clearly who we are. This is not a relationship which can be cobbled together as we see fit, because our view of marriage is distorted by sinfulness and false understanding.

There is also a fundamental religious dynamic to marriage. A humanist culture can construct relationships from its own sources of inspiration, but if these are suspect, then the consequent relationships will also be. The Christian faith recognises a given quality to them. The meaning of love, faithfulness, truth and intimacy comes from God, and those who cut themselves off from God lose the sense of what is the basis of this relationship and what these qualities mean.

Marriage is instituted by God

Let us for a moment reflect on the meaning of *institution*. It is a word loosely used within sociology, but its original meaning is Christian, as Calvin's *Institutes* convey. It denotes what God has said should be, and because God is Creator, it is fundamental to our lives. It is an inescapable part of life. The great marital institutional statement occurs in Genesis 2:24, 'For this reason a man will leave his father and mother and be united to his wife, and they will become one flesh.' This sentence from Scripture is one of the most powerful of all statements about human life. It also conveys the following themes. Men and women are made for one another. The common identity and attraction of man and woman compel each generation to unite. On maturity man and woman leave the family of origin and on their own initiative move to marriage. Marriage is a full personal union and it involves the uniting of bodies (without shame) and lives in one. This text reverberates through history and it shows an institution which is basic to all societies at all times; it is universal. Because we are created this way, the text inescapably addresses our existence. Marriage has a given structure which is well, or defectively, reflected in people's lives. So marriage is defined by norms like love and faithfulness which have a particular expression in this area of life. Marital love, in some respects, is different from parental love.

But the Christian meaning of institution can be misunderstood. Often 'institutions' are seen as social pawns which are manipulated by Society (Functionalism) or the State (Statism) or as forms imposed on people's lives (Structuralism). The external form is then contrasted with the internal dynamics. The biblical meaning is different; it penetrates to the lived subjective content of our lives. It divides soul and spirit, joints and marrow; it judges the thoughts and intentions of the heart. Thus the biblical norm of love searches us, opens up our lives, creates intimacy and allows us to find ourselves in marriage. It is not an external social imposition, but discloses our very inner selves.

Viewing marriage as instituted by God is slightly different from some other Christian approaches. Catholic and other views have seen it as *sacrament*, a view which emphasises the status of marriage before God but tries to make the Church and its rite – the wedding ceremony – central to the meaning of marriage (Schillebeeckx, 1965). This undermines the biblical understanding of the universal significance and importance of marriage over against a Church marriage service. Perhaps it has arisen because the Church has wanted to assert *its* importance for marriage. If God has validated marriage, nothing more is needed (Calvin, 1962, II, 646–9). There is no magic in the ceremony, just vows before God and an unqualified commitment to marriage which a couple then keep. Clearly the wedding service allows an overt recognition of the God-given nature of marriage and how it is to be lived, but it is not what makes a marriage. Later I will suggest that it is the right and best way to get married, but perhaps there needs to be a massive transfer of Christian attention from weddings to lived marriage.

Other Christians see marriage as a *covenant*, focusing on the biblical meaning of covenantal faithfulness (Atkinson, 1979). The Bible emphasises the similarity between God's relationship with the Children of Israel and faithfulness in marriage. But it is easy to interpret the meaning of covenant loosely as a covenantal relationship *between* husband and wife. The underlying biblical meaning is far more rigorous. God's covenantal relationship with humankind and the Children of Israel is fundamentally unequal. God the Creator is faithful and commands, and we responsively obey on God's terms. The marital covenant is not between husband and wife, but between the husband and wife together and *God*. This is powerfully stated in Malachi. 'You ask, "Why?" It is because the LORD is acting as the witness between you and the wife of your youth, because you have broken faith with her, though she is your partner, the wife of your marriage covenant' (Mal. 2:14). Thus the meaning of covenant conveys the character of the couple's relationship with God and not with each other. It is the prior relationship of life, including marriage, and for this reason an institutional understanding perhaps best conveys all that marriage means.

Marriage and family are two linked institutions

Marriage and Family are linked, but the former is not to be subsumed under the latter – a man *leaves* his father and mother and cleaves to his wife. The marriage has its own integrity, which should be reflected in the attitudes of the couple and of others. Parents should not intrude on the marriages of their children. Later, when children arrive, Husband and Wife do not become just Dad and Mum. Thus, a marriage without children has its own integrity of love and companionship. Distinguishing between the two institutions is crucial; we do it all the time. Nurturing, parental love is different in kind from reciprocal marital love. The *incest taboo* (Lev. 18) is a universal norm which conveys the fundamentally different nature of marital and family relationships; the first involves a sexual relationship, while the latter must not.

The biblical emphasis underlines how *marriage is the foundation for family*; mutual help, love, sexual union and procreation are the basis on which a two-parent family is built. This truth is significant within the dynamics of life. When a marriage is good, so will the family life be, simply because the two formative adults are right with one another. When a marriage is bad, it transmits all kinds of problems to the next generation.

This primacy of marriage has often been ignored in sociological literature. Many anthropologists and sociologists have thought of the family as a single institution within which sexual relationships and procreation are regulated by practices including marriage. Sometimes the assumption is that really we are just rutting animals, that instinct must be controlled by social mores and that marriage is just a convention of sexual control. Often there has been a family-centred interpretation of marriage. Radcliffe-Brown, Westermarck, Goode and Fletcher have tended to this view. More recently sociobiology has popularised the view that Nature drives procreation. Marriage is merely an uneasy compromise in the procreative impulse. Actually, few men are concerned as to whether their sperm are having a raw deal. Probably they never talk to them ... Perhaps these views all miss out on important insights about the structural relationship of marriage to family (Storkey, 1979, 225–8).

Marriage is one institution among others with its own integrity before God. It is not subsumed under the State, Economy or Church

There is also a biblical understanding of the place of marriage in the wider social structure. Because marriage is created by God as a unique structure for humankind, it has its own integrity and is not a pawn in wider society. The independence of marriage from other human institutions is thus a central principle. This theme is played out in one of the precepts of the Mosaic law. 'If a man has recently married, he must not be sent to war or have any other duty laid on him. For one year he is to be free to stay at home and bring happiness to the wife he has married,' (Deut. 24:5). Here marriage is not to be dominated by the State. Each institution has its own norm and purposes, and in each responsibility before God is central, not the dominance of another institution. This principle is reflected in the kind of guidance which Paul gives towards the end of his letters. He works out the implications of the Christian faith in various institutional areas – marriage, family, work and politics (Rom. 13; 1 Cor. 5–7; Eph. 5:21–6:9; Col. 3:18–4:1; 1 Tim. 5:1–6:10). These are seen as obvious areas of Christian obedience where norms of good living and wisdom are needed.

This understanding, reflected throughout the Bible, gives us a *pluralist* understanding of institutions which can be summarised in Figure 3.1.

This reflects the kind of argument developed by Mount (1983) in *The Subversive Family*. Marriage and family are institutions which stubbornly do their own thing. Provided we do not act unjustly, our marriage and family life are ours and reflect our freedom to live as we choose before God unbeholden to other institutions. Later we shall look at the relationship between marriage and these institutions, but the central biblical point is that all are open to and responsible before God and none is to be subsumed under the other. Marriage is not a tool of the State or of employment practices, but is couples living in open relationship with God. This principle, called *sphere sovereignty* by Kuyper, and part of the principle of *subsidiarity* within Catholic thought is an important structural understanding of the relationship of marriage and family to other institutions. Although non-Christians may not acknow-

Figure 3.1

ledge God it is possible for them, too, to live within its implications.

Within marriage each person continues to depend centrally on God's relationship with them, their partner and marriage

We now come to consider the inner structure of marriage, and here we face some crucial issues of world view. Broadly speaking, there are two non-Christian possibilities. Either the marriage is seen in terms of an individual who is self-referenced and enters into an external or contractual relationship articulated from the ego, or a partner identifies himself or herself within the marriage and in relation to the partner. The *self-directed* or individualist model has a pathology which was partly explored in the last chapter. Its egocentricity always leaves the relationship subsequent. The *other-directed* view means that one partner is religiously dependent on the other. It is a *wife-directed* or *husband-directed* marriage. All of these views contrast with Christian understanding.

Here marriage is not self-contained and self-referencing, but is open to God. Each partner has a relationship, identity and ultimate worth before God, who also recognises the union and relationship which constitutes the marriage. For the biblical teaching about marriage also involves a much more central point about the total meaning of life. Central to human existence is the relationship which each person has with God. In Genesis 2 and 3 it is quite clear that the man and the woman have a relationship with God. Eve, for example, acknowledges it in childbirth. 'With the help of the Lord I have brought forth a man.' (Gen. 4:1). But even where people do not recognise it, their existence and identity rest in the relationship the Creator has with them, and their responsive relationship with God, even though that might be one of indifference and denial. The central command of life is that 'You shall love the Lord your God with all your heart, soul, mind and strength, and your neighbour as yourself', and this feeds into the relationship of marriage. Thus, personal identity is not lost in marriage, because each person responds in faith in one way or another to God and to their partner. Thus, the basic model of marriage is not just of a pair, but of a pair each and both in relation to God (see Figure 3.2). This is the truth of our existence and the terms in which marriage relationships should be understood.

Here we understand the identity of each person – husband and wife – before God. Human identity is not lost in marriage. A person does not dissolve in a union, but enters into it. At the same time the union is acknowledged by and before God and has its integrity as marriage. The purposes and laws of God are clearly central to the marriage, and there is an inner link between a faithful response to God and faithfulness in marriage. These central points we shall explore in a more systematic way by identifying a set of

Figure 3.2

principles which define the created meaning of marriage in biblical terms.

Marriage is not the central meaning of life

This point is really an extension of the previous one. When human beings transfer the central meaning of life which is found in God to this human relationship, they lose the proper sense of life. Love is God-given, not partner-generated, and it must continue when the partner fails. There are other relationships in life which are important, and everything cannot be subsumed to the purposes of marriage. Paul warns about marriage which is self-referential, 'a married man is concerned about the affairs of the world – how he can please his wife – and his interests are divided' (1 Cor. 7:33). and he therefore relativises the significance of marriage. 'From now on those who have wives should live as if they had none; those who mourn as if they did not; those who are happy as if they were not' (1 Cor. 7:29–30). Life is not meant to revolve around marriage, but marriage may be part of our lives before God.

Again this understanding stands against the romantic tradition which tries to lift man–woman passion to the role of the basic principle or inspiration of life. The link between this ethos and tragedy in world literature should at least warn us of its problems. (Petrarch's *In Vita* and *In Morte di Madonna Laura*, Shakespeare's *Romeo and Juliet*, *Othello*, *Anthony and Cleopatra*, Goethe's *The Sorrows of Young Werther*, Keats's *La Belle Dame sans Merci*, Tolstoy's *Anna Karenina* and many other writings reflect this pattern.) At a more immediate level 'being in love' and 'life as romance' generate all kinds of problems, because everything is focused on love and marriage and other relationships are ignored or undervalued.

Marriage is a personal, voluntary, mutual commitment

Marriage is a *voluntary* commitment to share life with this other person. This means that in principle being single or being married are states which are equally good; it is just a matter of choice. No judgement can be made of one state over the other. Paul is incredibly direct on this issue. On the one hand he states, 'It is good for a man not to marry' (1 Cor. 7:1) and entirely vindicates singleness on the grounds that it allows wholehearted service of God, but on the other hand, he points out that those who 'forbid people to marry' are 'hypocritical liars whose consciences have been seared as with a hot iron' (1 Tim. 4:2). Either person is free not to marry and there should be no compulsion or pressure to make the choice from other people or from circumstances. Similarly, if a person decides to marry because of pressure from a partner, an existing sexual relationship, for money or status, or in reaction to things from the past, this compromises the full voluntary commitment. Declared choice is, of course, the fulcrum of the wedding service. It must be made on no other grounds than a voluntary commitment to be united with this person.

Arranged marriages contradict this principle in so far as parents control the decisions of their children. Many of course do not. The parents provide contacts, suitors or proposed partners and no more. But they may only allow a veto for the bride and/or the groom, or even deny that. It was the Reformation which established the principle of marital choice for men and women which has now become ubiquitous (and individualised) in the West. Some arranged marriages in Asia and the Middle East put cruel burdens on young couples. *Exogamy*, the requirement of marrying outside a certain group, and *endogamy* of marrying within groups, sometimes compromise the scope of marital choice.

The commitment must also be *mutual*. The idea of one person choosing to marry another is not good enough, because both must choose. It should also not be a choice of marrying from among a range of different possibilities, because this demeans the person who might be rejected. There are stages of development in the relationship. Going out, dating and friendship are stages when the question of *are we to marry* remains latent. Then the choice of whether to marry this person arises. Courtship, going steady, engagement and betrothal mark different stages of the process of proceeding to marriage. There is evidence that we have lost some of the sensitive stages of relationship development which have previously allowed couples to move gently towards, or away from, marriage. It should be a peaceful process, without pressure.

It is also *personal*. Because this is a self-giving of the whole person, it involves coming to a point of integrity. This needs a pure spirit, a full sense of selfhood and a wholeness of life. This is one of the main reasons why premarital sex is wrong; it undermines this wholeness and gives a person tensions between their body experience and their self-giving.

Prostitution, having a mistress or lover, and cohabitation (in varying degrees) compromise this principle by withholding some level of personal commitment while giving another.

Marriage is a choice to be made in maturity when a person has 'left father and mother' and is not still wrestling with the issues of selfhood and growing up

Marriage is for adults, for men and women who have moved from parental dependence and are exercising their personal choice. This implies a legal *minimum age* of marriage to protect persons from immature decisions and some degree of family and community support to reach this kind of maturity. There is a question of whether a person is ready for marriage, for the kind of commitment involved is deep. It needs to be made maturely, without impulse, with self-knowledge and when a person is collected and whole.

Maturity is a complex issue. For some who are embroiled in family and other personal problems which affect them deeply, it suggests that they should move through these difficulties before going to marriage rather than carrying them into the marriage. Sexual maturity is often wrongly defined in terms of physical maturity, when the real issue is whether a person can establish a tender, loving union with a partner for life. The sexual exploitation of the immature today is out of control and warped, a massive issue which needs addressing. Many have physical, social and economic maturity out of kilter.

Marriage is heterosexual, because men and women were created to enter into marriage together

Man and woman are created for one another as part of the richness of humankind, and the union of marriage is innately heterosexual, physiologically and in terms of the sharing of sexual mutuality. Marriage is instituted as the union of a man and a woman, reflecting the way we are created. In this way the mutuality of man–woman relationships is intimately expressed in each generation. This is especially important because alienated gender cultures easily develop between men and women, but here intimate sharing is built into our lives.

The Judaeo-Christian tradition has seen homosexual and lesbian relationships as antinormative and created by corrupt cultures. There may be reactive reasons why people move into same sex relationships, but they are denials of the biblical normative pattern for humankind. For a while homosexuality was seen as a natural condition with some physiological or biological base, but it is now increasingly clear that homosexual and lesbian experience is culturally generated, and these cultures can be questioned and do involve normative choices.

Marriage is monogamous

The central biblical understanding of marriage is *monogamous* – a man united with a wife and they become one flesh, one husband married to one wife. Only monogamy allows one partner to give themselves fully to the other. *Polygamy* – two or multiple partners – is problematic; it is properly seen as one partner trying to contract multiple marriages, but never fully able to do so. The most common form is *polygyny*, having more than one wife. Really, it was quite uncommon, because in cultures where polygyny was practised, it was so among only a small minority of men. Sometimes it occurred because male infanticide, murder and warfare reduced the number of men (Queen *et al.*, 1985, 53–68). It was often marked by men using economic and military power to obtain women, by women marrying young and by older polygamous men leaving young men single for a number of years. There were normally patterns of male power and female subservience. The destructive dynamics of this pattern can be seen in the personal history of Abraham, Isaac and Jacob in Genesis as well as in much other literature. It was usually marked by jealousy between wives, ranking of wives and concubines, cruelty by the senior wife, overworking women, rivalry between children, and by tension for the husband as he tries to cope with multiple relationships. Often, of course, the bonding with one wife was deeper, leaving the others lonely or bitter, although sometimes companionship among wives was good. The pattern was common in East and West Africa, China and Japan and other native cultures, but it has tended to atrophy through the influence of Christian standards. Islamic Shari'ah affirmed polygamy, with the husband having the right of up to four wives, but in recent years countries with a strong Muslim political presence have forbidden or limited polygyny (Doi, 1984, 144–54). Some Mormons affirmed polygamy between 1852 and 1890, but they, too, have disavowed it. *Polyandry*, a wife having more than one husband, was rare and seems to have been accompanied by female infanticide. It has now more or less disappeared (Queen, *et al.*, 1985, 17–35). Monogamy is not, of course, merely a matter of legality, but involves not entering into other marriage-like relationships.

Marriage is a union between a husband and wife. This means that each person gives themselves unreservedly to the other both initially and continually

This is the core of the biblical meaning of marriage. The union is *full personal sharing*. The whole of one person is given to the other and vice versa. Each relationship of marriage is full of the wonder and glory of the creation – the discovery of this one person. It is a sensitive process and in many marriages we are too familiar; we presume what we have not really discovered. There should be no fear of the other and no rejection by the other, but a commitment to share life and bodies together. Every area of life is to be shared, including sexual union. Union is not a loss of identity, but a sharing of personhood. It is helpful to consider the areas of life in which a couple is called to union.

Table 3.1

Area of life	to be shared	failure
Faith, culture	relationship with God, prayer, Christian or other faith response, view of marriage and views of life	indifference, privatised faith, basic clash of views
Ethics	views of morality and ethics, choices in life, principles, areas of ethical concern	moral, ethical barriers
Social Relationships	families of origin, friends, work and community relationships, attitudes to relationships	segregated friends, in-law problems, private friends or unshared relationships
Justice	sense of fairness and justice, political convictions, attitudes to power	unfair marriage relation, wider social injustice
Economic life	mutuality of work: paid, domestic, voluntary, home, property, shared resources, money, property, economic care of children, shopping, saving. Shared rest, giving	Private wealth. Unfair sharing of work, breakdown of economic trust
Education	Christian understanding, wisdom, academic knowledge, experience, skills. Shared teachers, insights, areas of awareness	Different understanding, no knowledge of what the other has learned. Unwillingness to learn
History	Personal and family history. Shared place in wider social history. Personal faith history	Undeclared history. Poor awareness of partner's history
Rest and play	Relaxation, sports, holidays, sleep, games and pastimes	Obsessive, individualist play, sports. Stress
Language and communication	Shared forms of discussion, verbal sharing, meanings, response to arts, media, newspapers, body language, Bible reading, verbal cultures etc.	Communication barriers and unshared languages. Faulty and hostile communication. Arguing and recrimination

Table 3.1 (Cont.)

Area of life	to be shared	failure
Aesthetics	View of beauty, dress, creation of home, attitude to colour, music, art and wider arts	Loss of sense of beauty and glory. Ugliness in marriage.
Thinking and analysis	Shared logic, levels of thought, perspectives, frames of reference, critical awareness and areas of special knowledge. Mutual thinking	Antagonistic ways of thinking. Barriers to discussion. Egocentric thinking
Psychology, emotions	Shared feelings, empathy, sensitivity, openness	Sense of loneliness, depression. Anger, not being understood. Detatchment
Body, biology	Care of bodies, sexual relations, health, sickness. Diet	Lack of body care. Unshared sex. Violence. Abuse
Geography	Home, travel, response to the area where we live, attitudes to transport	Spatially segregated lives
Energy	Abilities, commitments, physical energy	Chronic tiredness

This gives some idea of the potential scope of this union; it creates a drama for life as a couple opens up the one to the other, as fully as possible. A couple does not have to be the same in these areas, but to share differences, gifts or problems. The wife in a wheelchair is given and respects her husband's energy. There is thus a tremendous amount to share. There are no no-go areas. It is a life's work to open up to one another. Each stage involves new depths, new challenges, another aspect of union. In every area of sharing there needs to be love and respect that make the sharing easy and constructive. When there is an area of failure, it can easily feed back into the central relationship.

Marriage is characterised by love

Again, we are at the heart of the relationship. It is marked by love. Christian love does not just involve feelings, duty, sex and intimacy, but is a personal commitment which goes beyond these. It must be gentle, tender and patient, because these attitudes are required if we are to open up one to the other. This includes all the normal attributes of Christian love – patience, kindness, tenderness, protection, seeking the best for the other, not being rude, angry, proud or vindictive, but it also means cherishing this person fully for life whatever the circumstances. Marital love is also humble, counting the other as more important. Love goes through difficulties. It is rock solid and draws on the central truths of God's relationship with us and the rest of the universe. Love comes as a command to us, not so that it may just be a duty, but because this is the only way for a marriage to live (Kierkegaard, 1962; Allender).

Love is much misunderstood. It is not just feeling *based* and subjective. It is not to be focused in *my* happiness. It is not an ideal, but an everyday reality. It does not depend on compatibility and sameness, but can be expressed across differences. It is not something which we achieve, but which occurs in response and obedience to God. It is not a romantic worship of the other, but an actual response to another weak human being. It is not self-generated, depending on our whims and weaknesses, but comes from God's love for us and our response to God. It covers a multitude of sins and wins victories over failures. It is always *for* the other, and never *against* them.

Marriage is faithful

Faithfulness touches deeply who we are. Relationships which come and go say that we and others are disposable, cheap, of passing interest. Actually, any worthwhile relationship lasts. Friends stick. We are faithful to a good teacher whom we have not seen for twenty years. Mum will be there. Deep commitments are not brought to an end or withdrawn, but are given for life. Faithfulness reflects God's steadfast commitment to us in its quality and depth. God's steadfast love is with us through life and death. Paul states, 'For I am convinced that neither death nor life, neither angels or demons, neither the present nor the future, nor any powers, neither height nor depth, nor anything else in all creation, will be able to separate us from the love of God that is in Jesus Christ our Lord' (Rom. 8:38). Faith*ful*ness implies what it says. It must be full faith, not just in sexual relations, but in all areas of life. Private money, thoughts and even emotions are not on, because there is to be no *withdrawal* from the other partner. The relationship is meant to be, or move towards, complete openness. If faithfulness is there, *trust* will be, and vice versa. Trust is easy and simple. You know where you are and there is the space to relax and explore a relationship. Indeed, trust is one of the prime requirements of a good sex life; when a couple trust one another they can enjoy giving and receiving, but when one person might use the other, there is tension. Thus, faithfulness is the strong inner commitment which makes a marriage positive and affirming in its basic structure.

There is much in our culture which makes the idea of faithfulness difficult. Sometimes it is the pushing of self-gratificatory sex. It is also existentialist and consumer views of life. 'I can't make a long-term commitment.' 'My wants will change.' 'I need a range of experiences.' Individual choice rules in many people's lives but there is probably a deeper issue behind this. Life as a string of experiences hung together is often very fragmented and defeating. The 'I' who is behind an existentialist, pragmatic, hedonist or experientialist view of things is deeply confused. What we witness is a culture which has unthinkingly moved out a responsive relationship with God and at the same time a knowledge of self. Although a high proportion of the population believe vaguely in God, they often do not think and respond to God's faithfulness as their Creator and Saviour. The ground of our existence is God's faithfulness to us. It works through failings, weakness and even evil for our good; it is steadfast love. The agenda of marriage does not start with our faithfulness, but enters into the faithfulness of God Who makes the sun shine on good and evil alike. A heartfelt vow can, therefore, with God's help be kept for life. No husband or wife who unconditionally and regularly prays for their partner is likely to find faithfulness much of a problem.

Marriage is an exclusive sexual relationship or bodily union

Marriage is monogamous because the whole of one person is given to the whole of another. The sexual relationship expresses this and must therefore be exclusive; to give my body to someone else would be to lie and cheat. Second, because marriage involves receiving the body of this other person, to reject their body and go after somebody else is a disgusting form of rejection. Third, sex as a true expression of love involves a complete faithful commitment to the beloved. It is not possible for the same expression to be made with someone else. Just because love and marriage are full of longing and tender bonding, they are also rightfully jealous.

> Place me like a seal over your heart,
> like a seal over your arm;
> for love is strong as death,
> its jealousy unyielding as the grave.
> It burns like blazing fire,
> like a mighty flame.
> Many waters cannot quench love;
> rivers cannot wash it away.
> If one were to give

> all the wealth of his house for love,
> he would be utterly scorned.
>   (S. of S. 8:6–7)

It is because the passion of marital love is so great, that the jealousy of sexual unfaithfulness is so painful. Millions are suffering from it. Those who say it does not matter (usually those who commit it) are terminally hardened or pretending.

Yet sexual unfaithfulness has become more common, (and always been a problem). There are many reasons. Indulgent media presentations of adultery often reflect a self-justification of the private lives of the people involved. Faithfulness suffers extraordinary underexposure in the media. Premarital sex undermines marital faithfulness. The sex industries push consumer sex. Sometimes people actually believe that adultery is all right as long as the partner doesn't know about it. Some men are committed to predatory sex and harassment. The groaning weight of misery and emptiness caused by sexual unfaithfulness in our culture is so great that no one picks it up. We walk round it and look away to the series of myths which say it does not matter, the musack of lies.

Marriage is a relationship of equality and respect

Marriage has been seen at different times with the man or woman dominant but there are many different idioms for this pattern. He can be the Master, the Macho or the Manager: she can be the Mistress, the Venus or the Last Word. Really, these patterns are different from patriarchy and matriarchy which refer to family control, because they relate to the dynamics between the couple. *Husband or wife control* is a powerful dynamic. Both of these in Christian terms are pathologies. The great Creation narrative not only shows Adam as responding to Eve with the egalitarian 'Bone of my bone and flesh of my flesh!', but, as we have seen, quotes God as saying, 'I will make a helper suitable for him.' The word the Lord God uses is the word he ascribes to himself, ezer (helper), Ebenezer (God our help). This is partnership. The Scriptures then present the pathology of later patriarchal patterns and with Jesus the mutuality and equality of men and women are restored, not only in faith, but also in marriage. The emphasis is on mutual submission, as opposed to the exercise of power by one partner over another. In fact Jesus provides the most devastating critique of the use of power as domination that the history of the world has ever seen. Turning the other cheek and patriarchy don't go well together. Marriage is a union of equals, and the creation or use of power as domination usually means a breakdown in love.

This understanding of marriage has often been weak because of the ideologies and effective power of the male gender in marital relations. Physical, political, economic and even Church power have often been used to establish a culture of wife control. On the other hand, Churches have often provided a wholesome model of mutuality and respectful gender relationships which have had a deep impact on Western culture, a theme taken up by some branches of feminism, but it has also promulgated versions of male dominance. Hopefully, these are in retreat and the central biblical insistence on the equal status of men and women before God and the need for mutual respect and love in marriage are growing (Elaine Storkey, 1985, 1995).

Some Christian debate in this area has centred around the notion of 'headship'. This is a concept which some have seen in a number of biblical texts. The most famous of these occurs in Ephesians 6. Here the text says, 'Submit to one another out of reverence for Christ, wives to your husbands as to the Lord. For the husband is the head of the wife as Christ is the head of the church, his body . . .' (Eph. 5:21). Full study of the text cannot be carried out here, but a few points can be made. The clear central principle is mutual submission. But a subsequent crucial issue is what is Paul trying to convey by appeal to Christ as the head. There has been much debate about *kephele* focusing either on authority or source, but much of this debate on the word ignores the obvious focus of Paul's concern. He has already painted a very powerful picture of Christ as the head a chapter or so earlier. 'Instead, speaking the truth in love, we will in all things grow up into him who is the head, that is, Christ. From him the whole body, joined together and held together in every supporting ligament, grows and builds itself up in love, as each part does its work' (Eph. 4:15–6). Here, overwhelmingly, the focus is the union of the body and the head, on not being autonomous, but growing into Christ. This must surely be the focus in Ephesians 5:22. The emphasis is not on an authority relationship, but on the union of the wife with her husband – the central theme of Christian marriage. The elevation of this and other texts into some kind of authority principle (often using modern Western idioms of authority) thus wrongly compromises biblical teaching which is amazingly egalitarian, for example in 1 Corinthians 7.

Equality is difficult. The greatest difficulty comes from the cultural pride to control. Men know best; they must protect; they must control; they need rest. Real submission and humility before God which are reflected in humble and respectful gender relationships are still one of the greatest challenges on the planet.

These principles give us some kind of grasp on the created or structural meaning of marriage, what it is for human relationships. It is an understanding of marriage which is different from many sociological ones. These often look for common denominators which can be used to identify actual human relationships and eschew normative definition and understanding. But this perspective does not begin with the often confused and confusing relationships which are the result of human sinfulness and misunderstanding. The definition of marriage given above tries to identify its created character and what it is truly meant to be. By using this biblical understanding of healthy marriage, we can more easily see the pathological patterns.

4

MARRIAGE AND THE FAMILIES OF ORIGIN

Introduction

All of us learn at a furious rate from the families in which we grow. Children observe, reflect, respond and relate in response to their parents. The parents are the initiators, and the children the respondents, although with degrees of independence from a very early age. Today I saw a little girl of no more than three whose father pointed in one direction; she pointed in another, and her father eventually followed *her* finger. However, what is learned is difficult and complex. Much sociological literature talks about learned roles and socialisation, but these are only some of what children learn. In this chapter we shall try to explore some of the deeper aspects of what is learned from the families of origin about marriage, personhood, values, faith, culture and the ethos of family life. First we consider some general points about kinship.

Family and kinship

Family structures grow out of marriage, and depending on the kind of view of marriage, so family relations develop. The *conjugal family* where marriage generates family and kinship is the universal type. In cultures dominated by a family-centred view of marriage there is a strong difference between links from parents to children – *blood*, or *consanguineal relations*, and relationships based on marriage – *affinity relationships*. In family-centred systems the emphasis

tends to be on tracing the family line through blood relationships, *patrilineal* forms through the father or *matrilineal*
forms through the mother. In the West, largely under
Christian influence, the equality of blood and affinity
relationships has emerged in many families. Uncles and
aunts come equally from both sides of the family without
differentiation, and on the whole all *parent-in-law* relationships are seen as shared. In Britain there are many subtle
variations. In some areas the mother–daughter link is seen
as especially powerful, generating a mother-in-law problem
for the husband. In other families the mother–son link is
strong creating a mother-in-law problem for the wife. One
important trend in the West is from an *extended family*,
where there is strong interaction among the kin, to a *nuclear
family* where the conjugal unit is relatively isolated from the
rest of the family. Actually this trend is much more complex,
with a great deal of family interaction still occurring.
Another aspect of Western kinship is the pattern of *severed
kinship* which occurs through marital breakdown. The overwhelmingly most important relationships are, however,
those which occur through direct parenting, and it is to these
that we now turn.

Our parents' parents

It is a commonplace that we do not know our parents when
they were young. Yet often their deepest experiences and
views of life were formed in relation to *their* parents. Many
cultures preserve this history through local experience,
direct contacts between grandparents and children, and
repeated verbal family history. Often in Western cultures
we do not. Frequently when people research the early
relationship between their parents and the previous generation, they uncover things which explain what have previously been enigmas. The following are just some of the
problematic experiences which have been uncovered: war-

time bereavement and disability, family feuds, prostitution, the death and near death of an older child, wartime evacuation and cruelty, overcrowding, sexual abuse, emotional withdrawal, imprisonment, regretted marriage and childbearing, bullying, loneliness, maternal violence and a father absent through work for five years. Frequently, when the life of parents is seen in greater depth, all kinds of puzzling experiences fall into place. At the same time the life of our parents was frequently marked by joy and a great sense of happiness. They have had deep experiences of the glory of creation, tender care, important formative relationships with adults, the freedom of a childhood without cars, the delights of Sunday School outings and having a bath in front of the fire. They may have been in families which had no time for religion or where the Bible was frequently shared. Their Father may have been kind, never actually showed he loved them, always honest, put Grandmother first or come home from the war when Mum was three. Their Mother may have been constantly worn out, depended on Granddad, full of love and reassurance, always nagged or ignored in the family. And of course many of these reflections are not judgements, but memories of normal parental relationships remembered with the vividness of childhood. All of these experiences are carried through and reflected on in the lives of our parents. Each family has its own unique culture and values and we all can only later understand more of the parents we grew up with (Humphries and Gordon; Ten Boom; Hoggart).

One of the most important family experiences has been war. Almost every British family houses wartime tragedy. The First World War left over eight million dead, and many more bereaved parents, girlfriends, widows and orphans. Those patterns of bereavement stayed with people for decades. During that war there were also twenty-one million injured, often with permanent disabilities. More serious still for many of them was the direct experience of friends, comrades and supposed enemies dying and tortured by wounds. Often the results of the war were labelled, 'shell-shock', but they involved experiences which soldiers could not and did not want to share with anybody, because the horror was too great. The Second World War repeated this calamity, but at greater depth. One anonymous person remembers,

> My father had suffered during the war, and he rarely talked about it. One of the few times he did share his memories with us, he told of how their 'plane had crashed and he had had to cut his friend's foot off to get him from the wreckage. I'm sure the effects of the war must have had a profound effect on his life. Any faith that he may have had was, I think, destroyed in the RAF. It caused him to drink too much, and this coupled with the financial situation must have been the major contributing factor to the difficulties in the home in my early years ... My mother was four months pregnant with me when my sister had a near fatal accident. My father at this time was away at war. Subconsciously I may have been the last thing she needed.

This war was longer, from 1939 to 1945 and many stayed on in the forces in phased patterns of return to civilian life. Others were called up for National Service in the Korean and Vietnam wars. These long periods of separation have also been very important in the lives of many families. Death was yet more serious. It is estimated that between thirty-five and sixty million people died in the Second World War. Throughout the world families were defeated by death. Alongside the jolly nationalistic propaganda people suffered in their families. Jews faced the Holocaust and over ten million Russians died. There were mass bombings and other evils. Combatants suffered and tried to cope with the business of required murder. People lost their belief in God in the face of this human evil and horror.

Thus, the 1950s were not quite what they were portrayed. It was possible in the United States for some, perhaps, to be slightly removed from the war, but in Europe and elsewhere it ripped apart many marriages and families. Others were marked by anxiety, grieving, forced optimism and a quick resort to having a good time. The years after the war were marked by physical and psychological damage beyond what we can envisage. The question is how families recovered from this suffering, and the answer was that often they just tried to leave the past behind. In my childhood many families shared homes; we shared a home with my uncle and aunt. In many ways those years were marked by incredible reconstruction – rebuilding economies, families and institutions. In Britain many of the reforms were aimed at the young, giving them the resources to live good lives. Yet we do not know the full costs of the war. Men who had fought for five years and maybe worked excessively for a few more to rebuild the economy fathered the first rebel generation in the 1960s. And the ethos of war living was not good. Soldiers were pulled out of communities and learned to fend for themselves and have a good time. Married soldiers had affairs; there were poignant but passing relationships and the lost years were recovered through rushed courtship and a baby boom. Even now the children of Holocaust survivors are experiencing new kinds of suffering, so we can only guess how deep the problems and reactions were in the 1950s and 1960s.

But each age group is also quite specific in its culture. When we have grown up and lived is deeply significant. There is a set of other shared experiences which parents carry through life.

First generation migrant families
Thirties' depression children
Last rural generation
Baby boom children
National Service men
First generation house owners
Last extended family generation

First car owners
English working-class families
Black inner city children
First non-churchgoing generation
The first generation of nuclear family
First generation university children
The Sixties' generation
Reagan/Thatcher children
Television-raised children

Each of these is a bundle of experiences, insights or loss of awareness which is incalculable. We are now discovering that to have been a non-television child is something very special. But early life is also intensely personal. Here is one reflection.

At the age of 5 I started at the local primary school, which had been the village school attended by my mother as a child, only one mile from home. I fear I was an unhappy scholar and disliked school intensely. On my first day I was in tears, having forgotten to kiss my mother goodbye. The headmistress offered an obliging cheek for me to kiss instead, so I hit it! My mother was possessive of me, presumably conditioned by her experience. Certainly from earliest years I felt the world to be a big, dangerous place, populated by people who were, without exception, more worldly wise than me.

We need to know our parents and grandparents, if possible, at this kind of level. Every family should have its own detailed autobiographies where *who the family is* is shared with as much honesty and understanding as possible, so that we come to love our parents more, to understand and even escape from the experiences they have lived with.

Marriage – family – marriage

Parents are significant in many ways, but one of the chief ways is through their marriage. It is structurally important to the growing child. The two key people in its life are united and bonded by love. It gives the child a relationship outside itself which it must respect. It provides experience of each gender. It removes the child from feeling that the whole of life hangs on one human relationship. It means that its biological origin is love and tenderness. It provides the context of personal respect in which the child can grow. And it structures the child's experience of love. Because the couple love each other with adult give and take, the child can be dependent and receive love. He or she does not have to take on adult roles of loving. Thus the parental marriage is key – it is the basis of co-operation and mutuality out of which the child is nurtured and unconditionally loved.

There is more to this than we easily understand. If a marriage is a good union then the child will know that the husband and wife are *together* and share attitudes and understanding. Life will tend to make sense and normally this can be taken for granted. The daughter grows up trusting the togetherness of her parents and knowing their love as normal. There is sharing of work, emotions, home, bed, worry and decisions as a normal part of Mother and Father's marriage. She grows up within this and from the health of this relationship her own security emerges. It may scarcely be reflected on. The reality is that when the marriage is a good reciprocal relationship in which the couple give and receive from one another, false problems are not dumped on the child.

This is such a central principle that we must reflect on it more thoroughly. A marriage is a relationship which has its own integrity and dynamic. The man and woman should know mutual support and sharing. Their marital love and sexual intimacy should give them a union which is stable, peaceful and gives each of them respect and freedom before God. Even when there are problems, they should be sorted out between the couple concerned, if necessary with adult help. Yet it's a fair guess that something like a half of the problems of the world are ones *passed on by parents from their marriage to their children*. Anger, blame, cruelty, impatience, irritation and temper towards children are usually *scapegoating* processes from marriage relationships. The Bible seems obsessed with 'the sins of the parents being visited on the children', but rightly so, because of the scale of *dumping* which young children face. Jesus's words are yet more acutely addressed to this issue. 'If anyone causes one of these little ones who believe in me to sin, it would be better for him to have a large millstone hung around his neck and to be drowned in the depths of the sea' (Matt. 18:6). We thus acknowledge that the transmission of evil from the previous generation to us, and from us to the next, is a massive problem. Much of it occurs when *marital problems are falsely transposed into family ones*.

Let us tackle this same issue from the child's angle. Children grow up with an abundant amount of innate optimism and yet have problems like hunger, tiredness and colic. When these problems are solved, even if they are serious, they seem quickly forgotten or put in context. But children cannot understand many of the problems which adults have. They face them as Mum's continual worry, Dad's frown or ill-temper, an atmosphere, things that are never discussed or depression which has no reason. They cannot absorb that Mum did not want a baby, or Father is drunk and angry, or that promotion is the key to life or that Dad is sulking because he does not feel appreciated, partly because many of these issues are stupidly conceived by adults anyway. If Father has an affair while Mother is pregnant or neither parent is prepared to do the housework, the integrity of the child's life will be damaged, but the problem will be perceived as Mummy is always upset or a mess is normal. The meaning of these problems cannot properly be absorbed, and will tend to come out as the child's problems when clearly they are not. They obscure the simplicity and real innocence of childhood and prevent an infant from seeing their world with clarity. They may be naughty, but if the real problem is that Mum and Dad are naughty and are dumping on them, they have no hope of seeing things clearly. Because these problems are insoluble to the child, they often result in *transference*, the process where the adult responds in a false emotional way because of these early unresolved family relationships. Laing and others recognise severe forms of this problem as a source of schizophrenia (Laing and Esterton, 1970).

The parental marriage is also an example of marriage to the child. Here is where most of us learn what marriage is, how to love, the responsibilities, what kind of feelings to have, how to view husbands or wives. Of course, often we reflect on our parents' marriage and aim to change something, but the complexity of it often defeats us. We change what is in front of us, but at our back are the ways where we are the same. Or we react, but do not fully understand. The quip goes that when I was an adolescent, my parents were immature, but I was surprised by how quickly they grew up in the next few years. Where a marriage is seriously wrong, however, the children struggle in their view of marriage. They may approach their own marriage with fear, or face it as what seems to be an insoluble problem which makes them physically ill. They may expect to be unloved, or deserted, or veer into irresponsibility. They may be frightened of relationships which can generate so much stress. Most couples should tremble at the amount of emotional angst which we leave for our children to sweep up, or absorb.

The wife and her father

We now consider the four parental relationships which contribute to a marriage. The wife's parents' marriage says a great deal to her from an early age. The way her Father treats her Mother gives her one understanding of what it is to be a woman. She can expect to have respect and be given equal responsibilities with men. Her views can be dismissed and she can expect to be ignored. She will be 'decorative' or will be in charge around the home. She will be treated with intimacy and tenderness, or subject to aggression and irritation. Often these kinds of understanding will be seen as normal, especially if the father is dominant in imposing his kind of definition of the relationship, and it is only later that the daughter will learn to re-evaluate these assumptions and may grow out of them.

A good Father–Mother relationship will give her confidence that she, too, later in life can be loved, respected and honoured as a person. It will also mean that she does not expect gender tension generated by men through domination and assertiveness, but knows that women and men are both respected as adults. Marriage can be approached with confidence. A Father who treats a Mother badly will convey to the daughter that she, too, is growing up to this kind of life, and she may approach adulthood with an underlying fear or depression about marriage or an assertiveness that things 'will be different for me', that mating has to be a fight.

The direct Father–Daughter relationship is also important. Fathers who love their daughters and enjoy their company offer them a good understanding of themselves. This especially happens out of the security of a good parental marriage. The Father should give the daughter an easy sense of concourse between the sexes and an understanding of her own integrity before God and within the family. Sometimes fathers treat their daughters as mother, servant, coquette, ornament, of lower status, not needing education or not needing to develop views and understanding; clearly these roles dishonour them. There can also be an inside for girls/ outside for boys bias. Other fathers maintain a great social distance from their daughters, are very wary of showing affection, and withdraw fully when they reach adolescence, so that daughters experience the withdrawal of their father's love. Sometimes a fear of sexually predatory young men induces a strong attempt to discipline and protect the young woman, which a daughter cannot easily understand, let alone appreciate. Studies by Shere Hite and others convey how strong is the need among daughters for a good, open, honest relationship with Dad (Hite, 1995).

One principle which underlines this relationship is the *incest taboo*. This is spelt out in Leviticus 18 as an absolute requirement which shows the proper structure of marriage/ family relationships. Here mature voluntary sexual relationships take place between husband and wife within the union of marriage. This love has a different character from the nurturing of children, who are not sexually mature and cannot make sexual choices without manipulation. Marital sexual relations must not spill over into parent–child relationships. Parent–child incest dishonours the child's own right to mature sexual decisions and abuses the trust of a child. Fathers and stepfathers are the biggest problem. There are about six thousand children on registers for sexual abuse in England and the actual scale of the evil must be much wider. There should be none, but the principle is deeper than this. A parent should not compensate for weaknesses in the marital relationship by forming quasi-marital *emotional* ties with the child. This enmeshes the child in a relationship with the parent which is inappropriate. It also compromises other family relationships, especially that between Father and Mother. In most families there is just a basic understanding of the way relationships are conducted. A daughter should know complete sexual integrity within the family.

Probably, in most societies, this is the most neglected relationship of the four. Fathers tend to leave their daughters to their wives, when they should give love, affection, conversation and good male experience to their daughter. A good father will normally help a daughter to enter a good marriage at the right time.

The wife and her mother

Who her mother is can touch close to the identity of many women, but we must not overstate the case. The idea that people require and live in adult models is a very defective one. A daughter has her own identity before God, learns from both mother and father, and is herself. But much of the daughter's thinking, reflection and self-understanding will focus on her mother. Here all kinds of messages can be conveyed. 'It's your father who is important, not me.' 'We're on the same side and it's men that are the problem.' 'To get your way in this world you have to nag and shout.' Part of the scenario here is that often mothers have been very deeply identified with a role – of looking after, caring, doing housework, shopping and cooking, and the daughter also can feel she is growing into a role. But a role is not a person, and the deeper understanding of who her mother is remains elusive to the daughter. Does she have a faith, ambition, what values does she hold, why does she believe that? There are many mothers who in looking after their daughters in a wholehearted way still do not share themselves as fully as they could.

Mother is, of course, of the same gender, and gender learning often happens here. Many daughters have spent a long time listening to their mothers talk with other women. They learn what talking is like. A daughter learns from her mother whether education is important, what men are like, what kind of paid employment to seek, what is the purpose of activities within the home, how to look and what emotional vocabulary is appropriate. Especially she learns how to view marriage. Some mothers run matriarchal families; they find ways of exercising power over other members of the family, including the father. Clearly a daughter may learn this; it may be a source of tension during adolescence as competing patterns of control emerge, or the daughter may be treated as an ally. Many mothers and daughters are, of course, good friends, and mothers learn that being good friends involves respecting the marriage and relating as fully and openly to the son-in-law as to the daughter. But in other cases the mother encourages collusion against the men in the extended family, *gender collusion*. Here the husband faces a mother-in-law problem which is normally experienced as interference and a process of male exclusion.

Sometimes the dynamic of the mother–daughter relationship is weak. If the mother competes with her growing daughter in appearance or for attention, the rivalry will be destructive. Similarly, if a daughter believes in youth, beauty and education in ways which try to eclipse her mother, the relationship is harmed. Sometimes teen magazines and other media forms try to distance teenage girls from their mothers, and so there are many pitfalls for this relationship. It is possible for mothers to underestimate the intimacy, tenderness and care which daughters continue to want from their Mum and for Mum to continue in the earlier struggles of childrearing which are now obsolete (Friday, 1977).

The husband's father

It is easy for the Father to be seen as a kind of role. People often talk about a boy needing a *father figure*, but in my experience this term tends to be used when there is already distance or breakdown. In patriarchal societies this relationship has often been very formal, and this has been accompanied by the need for the father to be right. *Patriarchal distance* from children, including sons, sets up a particular pattern. Kids are for women, and only with some kind of *male initiation* does the son become a 'man'. Kipling's *If* and many other initiation rites convey this change well. Sadly, the whole process is built on gender distance and imbalance in parenting. British public schools have often institutionalised this pattern. A boy is not taken into maturity and adulthood, but through a gender loyalty conversion. This model leads many fathers to withdraw from the intimacy of early parenting. The biblical model of both parents being alongside a child in responding to God's ways is much better. When a father can be wrong and be forgiven by his children, he is in a much broader place.

What matters is not the father's performance, but the actual relationship – its unconditional love, commitment, faithfulness and patience. The son learns, grows, develops before God with the father as equal as a child of God. The father is also, equally with the mother, the one who cares for and teaches the boy, helping him to grow to maturity before God. Fathers should be part of the trustworthy, intimate development of the son's life. The son is not the father's possession, but has his own identity before God. Domination and control should not be part of fathering, and the son should easily grow up as his own person. The dominated son and daughter tend to rebel during the teens to establish themselves against the control, or perceived control. (For today the culture makes all constraint on the rampant individual seem like deep persecution.)

From the father the son learns many lessons about marriage. Many of them are unspoken. What kind of respect does he have for his wife? How loving is he? How does he express love? Is he faithful, not just in a technical sense, but in all his attitudes and commitments? Here there are potential disaster areas. A son can learn impatience and irritation. He can learn not to communicate. Anger and violence expressed by the father can undermine the son's self-control at an early stage. He can learn to be preoccupied by work. A son will know if a father is sexually unfaithful in practice or by intent, and may even absorb the father's patterns of self-justification.

The mother–husband relationship

Many sons have related to their mother as the caring and tender part of their parenting experience. Mum is the one who looks after me. Sometimes they have seen their mother as the emotional home, while the father is the achiever, the disciplinarian and the source of power. This old style caring relationship had many good qualities, but sometimes it involved the son *separating* in order to enter the competitive adult male world. Again, if the adolescent male's attitude to girls and sexuality and dating was one which implicitly dishonoured the mother, there was likely to be a gender barrier emerge. But this kind of relationship is often changing. Many women are going out to work, sharing all aspects of parenting fully, using childcare facilities and experiencing patterns of distance from their sons and daughters which have more rarely occurred before. Guilt, stress, competition, ineffective worry and distance emerge in ways which the mother and the son find difficult to handle. But the old needs are there for a caring tender, respectful relationship where the love of the mother is respected and returned, and the son shares his love.

Sometimes *Oedipal theory* is brought forward to suggest some kind of competition with the father for the mother's affection. With a good parental marriage relationship, the son should feel no competition for his mother's affection. He should also not feel his mother transferring any of her marital affection and emotional commitment to him, for that distorts the relationship, and can lead to the son being tied into his mother relationship in ways which inhibit his own dating and marriage. Here is the girlfriend's or wife's mother-in-law problem.

Parental deficit and hunger

Children's relations with parents should be good, rich and wholesome. They should know love and acceptance as their birthright, but today on a massive scale throughout the West, this is not happening. As marriages are breaking up, at a variety of different ages, children are losing their parents, mainly their fathers. Children also lose parents in a less traumatic sense through overwork, going off to boarding school, work away from home – many areas have migrant fathers aplenty, war, shiftwork and emotional absence. First, we need to understand what actually happens in these circumstances, for the adult perception is wrong. Adults often see a situation in terms of the need to have a divorce and then sort out care of the children. The children rightly see one parent as leaving them; they may not be sure which parent has caused the other parent to leave, but they have been rejected. Normally half of absent parents lose contact with their children more or less completely and for many others the contact is weak or limited. The children are correct. *They* are being left and rejected by the (effective) leaving parent. The crushing nature of this move for both spouse and children needs to be appreciated. A child who is known intimately is effectively told, 'You are not good to live with and I cannot love you as you are.' To be told this by one's biological parent is devastating. No child should be, for it is not true. The problem lies with the parent.

There is now abundant research showing the effects of this breakdown. Initially children may deny that the breakup has occurred. They may fantasise, have nightmares, live in fear that the other parent will leave. They will fear being left, cling and will try themselves to bring their parents together. Schoolwork will deteriorate and all kinds of other behavioural problems will arise. The child's own sense of rejection will often be overwhelming, and they will worry for and be angry at the other parent. The effects do not quickly disappear but will last through to the child's twenties when they too face the kind of relationship they will have. Sometimes the fear of relational failure will even make the person ill. But here we must note one overwhelming aspect of this trauma. It is the growth of *parent hunger*. The absence of the parent sets up a deep yearning which will often not be fulfilled in the child's development. The result, in a substantial number of cases, is that the child seeks relationships often with peers, homosexual or heterosexual, which are basically trying to meet this sense of hunger for intimacy and an open, unconditionally accepting relationship. Many of these relationships, because they have a false agenda, are more or less bound to fail.

Of course, children grow up and learn that what they have understood about themselves from their parents and of marriage from their parents may be wrong. However, it takes time for these lessons to work through. Children find out beyond the pattern of rejection that they have their own worth. The truths of God's care and love and of the sanctity of their own personhood seep through into experience and the view of the world, but they may marry late. The depths of these problems we do not understand.

Faith and identity

Thus, the way children grow up and the relationships they have with their parents are crucial. These go through many changes and dynamics. But growth should be into personhood where the child experiences her or his own integrity before God and this transition into maturity is important. It is not escape from parents, for that should not be necessary. Nor should it be escape into individualism and some kind of conception of self-focused freedom, for adulthood is full of responsibilities. Rather, the transition should reflect a sense of created worth and integrity, of maturity and selfhood before God which allows a person to choose to marry or not to with freedom. Families can give or withhold that sense from their children. Really, it is their birthright, because parents are only stewards of their children.

5

FRIENDS, DATING AND MATING

Friendship with trust

Friendship is often ignored in our culture, or is seen as second best to marriage and sexual relationships. The pressure to rush to sexual relationships often compromises the crucial position which friendship has in people's lives. Here we must explore it in relation to dating and marriage.

Friendship has a similar structure to marriage, but in many ways it is a more flexible relationship. It is a direct unique relationship between persons which is characterised by love and faithfulness. It is meant to be a relationship of patience and trust which always hopes and perseveres. Each person is to be kind, to delight in the good of the other person and to keep no record of wrongs. Of course, many friendships survive on far less than this. The relationship is not functional or shaped by roles, involves no authority relationships and is entirely voluntary. Friendship can cross all barriers of age, class, race and religion and can be part of any relationship which people form. Thus, it is possible to be friends with the policeman, the caretaker or the bus-driver. Here, therefore we have a relationship which is not meant to be reduced to less than a fully personal one. It is also not exclusive in the sense that having other friends does not compromise the relationship.

Its weight in human affairs can be gauged from the central place which Jesus gives it. Shortly before his death and resurrection Jesus explained that the character of his relationship with his disciples was that of friendship. He contrasted it with the more distant servant or employee, who did what he was told, but did not share with his or her boss. By contrast, Jesus indicated that he had shared everything of God the Father with them. It was an open relationship which Jesus had established in terms of friendship by choice. Jesus's *command* was that they should love one another – that friendship love should be the unequivocal basis of their relationship. The meaning of this love Jesus made very pointed, because he defined it in terms of being prepared to lay down one's life for a friend (John 15:9–16). Friendship is thus marked by love, faithfulness, joy and sacrifice, and it is to be the defining characteristic of the Christian community.

Friendship thus has its own integrity. It is good to be friends and is part of the sharing of life. Of course, there are good and bad friends. This is because the norms of friendship can be ignored or undermined. Friends should not flatter; they are not swayed by money, they love at all times and they tell the truth when it hurts. Many of us are bad or indifferent friends, but the relationship can continually be redeemed – friends can be forgiven; they can be loved through differences and even hate. We can be friends with anyone, and although the relationship should grow and have mutual depth, it is often possible for one person to sustain it. We can see this in Jesus's friendship with Judas. When Judas left the Upper Room to betray him, Jesus conveyed the step Judas was taking, but did not expose or attack him, and when Judas came to the Garden of Gethsemane still the friendship remained. A crowd of soldiers and others armed with swords and clubs came to Jesus. Judas stepped out and kissed Jesus, the act of friendship which was the prearranged sign of betrayal. Jesus, of course, knew and could see what was going on, but his response to Judas is, 'Friend, do what you have come for' (Matt. 26:50). Even when the treachery is clear, Jesus firmly insists on recognising Judas as friend.

But friendship is different from marriage. Friends can be of either gender; marriage is heterosexual. Friends retain the sexual integrity of their bodies; marriage partners share them. Friends are not exclusive; marriage involves forsaking all other. Marriage is a union, but friends do not share all of their lives with each other. Friends do not have children, but couples do. We must beware of making false comparisons. I do not think that we have grounds for saying that the marriage relationship is deeper than friendship; the depth of a relationship depends more on its openness to God. Jesus was not married and relativised the significance of marriage (Matt. 22:30) so the Scriptures do not allow us to put marriage in a hierarchical relationship over friendship. They are just different.

This preamble is important for several reasons. A lack of good friendships often impels people towards marriage *in order to find friendship*; if this occurs, it is a problem. Second, knowing the integrity of good friendships with both sexes is a good and important preparation for marriage; to be impelled from loneliness into an intense intimate relationship can create problems which need longer to solve. Third, friendship can be compromised by sexual relationships. Friendship should be voluntary and reciprocal, but genital intimacy can ruin this by changing the basis of the relationship and making it false. Further, friendship should be based on a stable sense of identity before God and a willingness to welcome and share with others. This kind of maturity is even more necessary in marriage where patterns of dependence, a quest for self and non-acceptance can create severe problems. In a sense, therefore, our friendships should act as good barometers of our maturity for marriage.

And there are bad friendships. Sometimes friends collude in violence, hating others, gossip and snobbery. Often friends are moulded to approve of faults and wrongdoings. They can be consumption-centred rather than personal. Sometimes one partner dominates or manipulates the other, and all kinds of dishonesty and insincerity can appear. They can be routine or excitement-seeking. The values which are built into, or absent from friendship, are one of the great shaping factors of life.

Premarital sex

One of the longstanding conflicts in Western culture has
been in the views of sex and premarital chastity. The
Christian attitude is that sex is reserved for marriage and all
premarital sexual relationships are wrong. I hold that view
and will argue for it later, but we first identify another
attitude, which is to believe that premarital sex is alright.
The traditional Christian view was the cultural norm, but it
is possible to overstate its impact. Premarital chastity was
often not observed. Among British men and women growing
up between 1935 and 1949 80 per cent of the men and 50
per cent of the women had sexual intercourse before marriage or engagement (Wellings, 1994, 74). Earlier the figures
were probably lower, but the two attitudes have been
around for a long time. Many men had a 'double standard'
whereby women were expected to be chaste, but they were
not, and this was reflected in the availability of some women,
prostitutes and others, to be sexual partners to those men.
Sometimes chastity was a fight. In Southern Europe young
women were kept indoors or heavily chaperoned in order to
protect them from predatory males. Often aristocratic males
abused female servants, and there is a hidden history of rape
and male sexual aggression. Nevertheless, the norm of
premarital chastity was probably accepted by a substantial
majority of the population in the nineteenth century. The
reasons were wider than acceptance of immediate Christian
authority. Young women were frequently told that if they
became sexually experienced they were likely to be used by
a variety of men and seen as a slut. The big danger was
pregnancy without a father, and without a good father. A
shotgun marriage was not great for the girl if she did not
want this man. Girls were warned against boys who wanted
sex but no commitment. There was also local knowledge of
sexual perverts who within and outside the family messed
up the lives of the young and weak if they could. Parents

and others used fear as a way of turning young people off sex – 'masturbation will send you insane'. More positively, men also looked to working and providing a home for a woman whom they wed, and they understood that they could not adequately grow to this responsibility while chasing girls. Sexual diseases were (and are) transmitted by extramarital relationships. So the norm of marital sex was sometimes upheld more by fear than chastity. But chastity was important. That you commit yourself to one person for life and share your body with them alone was understood by almost all the population as a norm, and a good one.

At the same time various aristocratic and avant-garde groups developed an ideology of open extramarital sex, possibly to justify their existing practices. Most of these groups were counter-cultural, but there is now a dispute as to what was going on among them. The progressive views of Annie Besant, Havelock Ellis, Sigmund Freud, Marie Stopes, Bertrand Russell among others were that they were pushing back the impact of repressive sex and allowing people the freedom which they did not have in a moralistic culture. Foucault and others have questioned this view. Foucault suggests that people in this tradition were themselves sexually obsessed, involved in the *hysterisation of women's bodies*, which led them to remove sex from its normal place in people's lives and invite others to their own obsessions. Certainly Ellis's interest in bizarre sexual activities like intercourse with dead bodies seems obsessive to me. And later writers in this tradition like Alex Comfort, Alfred Kinsey, Masters and Johnson can be seen as publicising and giving ideological justification to their own sexual journeys rather than being 'liberators'. Their approach was also different. Sex was a technical matter of physical stimulation, and cultural and religious norms were to be seen as an afterthought to the physical process of having sex (Masters, Johnson and Kolodny). This became the basis of sex education in schools, where questions of the character of relationships were often marginalised compared with techniques of contraception. But the critique of moralism also had weight; premarital sex was often declared wrong, but rarely was it explained why. Usually, as also with D. H. Lawrence, there was some vision of the purifying or religious nature of sexual experience. With the post-war popularisation of premarital sex, often carried out for commercial reasons, unchastity was propagandised to generation after generation.

For a while the technology of contraception seemed to allow the advocates of sexual freedom what they wanted. But a number of contradictions arose. Contraception, we were definitively told, would eliminate unwanted conceptions, but the number of abortions has *grown* over the last quarter of a century from well under 100,000 to a steady 160,000. Aside from the wrong of having these fetuses murdered, we ask why this technology has produced the opposite effect from that envisaged. At the same time the attitudes which were feared in earlier periods have become more prevalent. Predatory males, sex without commitment, transitory relationships are more common. Here we face the nub of the social problem. Sexual activity is easily distorted by human selfishness, aggression, dishonesty and lust, and without addressing these problems of human sinfulness in relationships, the problems grow. This cultural attitude has become dominant largely through commercial pressure rather than argument. When media empires promote lack of respect for women, the unqualified need for sex, media incitement to sexual arousal and sex-centred relationships, the quality of premarital relationships is bound to deteriorate. Commercial interests push for money-sex, image and compulsive relationships, and these tails have wagged the liberal ideological dog of non-repression. They feed kids the garbage of cheap sex to maintain their profit-sick world, wearing the fig-leaf of artistic freedom.

But this still leaves the question which each young person faces of whether and why premarital sex might be wrong.

We are all given the integrity of our bodies and the sexual integrity of the immature should never be used by older people; so there is a question of at what ages sexual intercourse is right; it needs maturity. But more than this, if sex is an expression of unconditional commitment, love and openness towards the partner, it must not be a lie. We must tell the truth with our bodies. The body giving must be real, because this is a precious, intimate relationship. Being truthful requires intercourse to be limited to marriage. If sex means 'It's OK for now,' or 'I want some fun,' or 'Your body, but not you,' or 'I'm making love to you, but later I may find someone else,' or 'I'm sexually aroused, but this doesn't imply anything about our long-term relationship,' then it is basically dishonest. The dishonesty always costs in terms of hurt, hardness and disillusion in the other person, and a knowledge of dishonesty within one's own body. Paul puts it graphically. 'Flee from sexual immorality. All other sins a man commits are outside his body, but he who sins sexually sins against his own body ... Honour God with your body' (1 Cor. 6:18–20). Sexual truth therefore occurs within an unconditional union of love, self-giving and permanence, i.e. marriage, and it cannot occur within premarital sexual relationships, because the commitment is not there. Outside marriage it generates the problems of deception and self-deception which follow from lying about true love. But true love, not cheap love, is what most of us want.

Of course, many young people see a different route through this issue. They are taught (normally by exploiting money-lovers) that sex is just about personal enjoyment and pleasure. It's a question of finding someone else and having fun. The sadness of this approach is that what should be an intimate relationship of human sharing becomes in principle and often in practice a lonely search for self-gratification. Even when in bed together, partners are really alone. This person cannot be trusted, may not be here tomorrow and I do not really matter to them. This is just a gratifying experience. There is more loneliness in bed than this world dreams of. Such a way of seeing things is no different in principle from the lonely pornography addict seeking an illusory form of sexual gratification. It is time, therefore, that the falseness of self-gratificatory sex, which tries to treat the other person impersonally, is exposed for its shallowness, and the necessary location of true sex and love within marriage is recognised.

There are also other issues which surround this question. The proportion having first sexual intercourse before sixteen is 28 per cent for young men and 19 per cent for young women – here the man is acting unlawfully (Wellings, 1994, 42). The median age is now seventeen for men and women. Younger women are likely to have first sexual intercourse with an older, sexually experienced man and probably a great deal of exploitation and manipulation occurs (Ibid., 68–70). We note that first intercourse was seen as being too soon by a growing number of younger people – 16 per cent of men and 37 per cent of the women between 16–24, although the majority felt it was about right (Ibid., 75). The main factor in first intercourse was curiosity, getting carried away, peer group pressure or being drunk for half the young men and 40 per cent of the young women – a bit circumstantial. Some 20 per cent more of the young women thought they were in love than the young men and presumably were quickly disillusioned (Ibid., 75). We do not know what the relationship between premarital sex and post-marital adultery is. It may well be complex, but it is also not likely to be negligible. It is time to acknowledge the extent to which premarital sex is problematic, and chastity is good.

Dating pressures

Often people experience external and internal pressures to present themselves as an attractive potential mate. Many social experiences for the young are essentially display routines as debutante, cheer leader or sportsman. The underlying idiom which they construct is a competitive pattern of mating in which each person tries to present themselves as especially desirable and to get to know someone who is a good catch. Often this pattern has strong cultural shaping. It used to have a class, status or caste component. Marrying above or below your class was wrong. Some parents have wanted to marry their children to someone who is rich, has a good job or 'has prospects'. The young often grade one another on looks, sense of humour, education or street credibility. Sociologists talk of *hypergamy* and *hypogamy*, the wife marrying up or down. The suffering that is caused by many of these competitive labels is beyond knowing, and it is easy for those in the mating game to be captured by or bowed by this kind of judgement. Actually, the process of mating is far more subtle than this. On the whole, mating grows out of the quality and depth of relationships, not out of shallow characteristics. There is no need to buy into this mode of dating.

A more serious problem for many today is moving from the anonymity of relationships into something with depth. The old pattern of marrying someone from next door, school, church, dance hall, the local youth club or the Young Conservatives has largely given way as these communities have become less formative and mobility has increased. College and work have become more significant. Deliberate dating agencies, advertised meetings, ways of going out, computer dating and disguised dating agencies have partly moved in to fill the superficial nature of many cross-sex contacts and allow relationships to develop. Many young people do not have friendship networks out of which deeper relationships can grow, and often peer groups have quite antagonistic attitudes towards the other gender and to the dating patterns of their own members. Girls can be catty towards a dating friend, or boys jeer at a mate going out with a girl. Because there is no clear distinction between friendship and a sexual relationship the whole set of dating contacts is fraught with fear, distrust, rampant emotion and a weak sense of allowing relationships to develop towards marriage or friendship.

There are other mating pressures. One is towards *homogamy*, the process whereby people marry those like themselves in age, height, race, job, education, religion or eating habits. On the one hand this may show how strong are the pressures to conformity in our intimate lives. On the other it may reflect shared values. *Exogamy*, the requirement of mating outside a particular group, normally only applies to immediate family in the West. Another tighter pressure may be to *endogamy*, marriage within a particular group. Here persons are required to or expect to marry other Jews, Catholics, Young Conservatives, Ivy Leaguers, Montagues or Capulets, Jets or Sharks. Often here the pressure comes from families, tribes or nations and reflects deep racial or cultural divisions which marital love is not allowed to cross. Not surprisingly, the great stories of Ruth and Boaz, Romeo and Juliet, Tony and Maria in *West Side Story* show the fight of love over endogamy. Clearly relationships which are *heterogamous*, which marry across boundaries, need the space, security, peace and love to work through the differences without requiring one partner to do all the conforming. There are many cross-cultural relationships where this has been done with great success and the richness of the resulting relationship has been all the greater.

There are norms of dating and mating. Dating for sex is demeaning and hurtful, even if both partners understand what is going on. Dating which is uncommitted and does not have a more focused intent should remain good friendship. Dating should not be competitive, pitting one person against another, and it should not move on to the state of possible marriage with more than one person at a time. It should allow freedom from being pressured into commitment, so that each respects the right of the other to choose or not choose them as partner. Usually, there is a stage of *engagement* or *betrothal*, where a couple understand that they are committed to one another and move through to know one another well enough to be committed to marriage for life. The sensitivity, respect, sharing and learning which are required in this process are way beyond what most couples give it.

Singleness

Singleness, like marriage, may be voluntary. Christianity has always seen the single and married state as having equal status. Jesus was not and could not be married. He is not a straightforward example for us in this, but he signifies that the most important things in life are not identified with the state of marriage. Indeed, Paul warns quite pragmatically about the wants of a marriage partner distracting husband or wife from the affairs of God and sees it as a troublesome state in the time when he was writing. A Christian understanding emphasises that living life in its fullness before God can be done single or married, but perhaps most easily in the former state. 'Are you unmarried? Do not look for a wife [or a husband]' (1 Cor. 7:28). Thus, Christianity does not see singleness as problematic. Barth and Brunner see marriage as in some sense higher because it incorporates the fullness of humankind as man and woman, but this is realised in many other ways than marriage, and it is no general argument. Singleness is thus a free mature state which should involve joy, contentment and a full sense of purpose before God.

Some may not feel that this is the case, although we all have periods of singleness as children, young adults, through widowhood or other circumstances. Many may not see singleness as voluntary. They have been refused marriage or not asked. This may be because singleness is seen as reflecting on them as a person, which it may. Many of us, single and married, are rude, angry and unpleasant; spouses often tell their partners that they should never have got married. The issue here is not being single or married, but whether there are things in our lives which need sorting out before God. Nevertheless, the feeling of being unwanted can be crippling, leaving people lost in self-pity and a burden of isolation. Here perhaps the cause of this sense is often misunderstood; the single person identifies it with themselves, but actually the problem often lies with marriage. Married couples are supposed to be happy ever after. Actually, four in ten of these relationships break down and a hunk of the others have serious problems. It is probably very difficult for married couples with these kinds of problems to expose their relationships to single friends, and so what single people often experience arises from the weakness and fragility of marital relationships leading to their own exclusion. If the myth were exposed, and the truth established that both marital and single relationships need love, care and patience growing from God's grace in our lives, we'd all be better off.

Singleness involves freedoms, patterns of flexibility and energy, the ability to give oneself more totally and the ability to have a wider set of relationships than those linked into spouse and family needs. It needs a good sense of self-love and self-respect. It should involve friends and neighbours who give community and sharing. It should be marked by a good sense of bodily integrity and intimacy in relationships. In every respect single people face all the challenges and blessings of life which are faced by married people. There is no difference between us. In our culture sometimes single people are exploited, labelled and used, but that reflects the weakness of marital culture. Actually singleness is now becoming more normal. The proportion of single person households in Britain has doubled from 14 per cent in 1961 to 28 per cent in 1995.

Pressures to marry or run from it

There are a variety of reasons which people can have which tend to push them into a marriage relationship on terms which are less than the full voluntary self-giving.

- People run away from troubled homes and express the need for parental love in a marriage or cohabiting relationship. They can run away from quarrels, abuse, disapproval or their own poor treatment of their parents.
- A sexual relationship has a fairly strong inbuilt pressure towards effective marriage. It often undermines the real choice.
- Sometimes a person seeks to 'find themselves', or to solve a range of personal problems through marriage. The issues are merely postponed.
- Sometimes people wish to settle down, get married, have children, without having the commitment to the other person.
- Marriage can be seen as escape from boredom, a dull job, from poverty and even from the cooking, rather than as love for the partner.
- It can be seen as filling a range of psychological needs – getting attention, meeting loneliness or owning someone – which tends to close up the relationship later.

Others avoid marriage for a similar range of reasons.

- The failure or tensions of the parental marriage leave them fearful of entering into their own marital relationship.
- The need for independence and control of lifestyle rules out commitment to sharing the life of another fully.
- Something is being hidden which seems impossible to share with another. Usually, it is not.

- An individualistic lifestyle has created barriers towards shared living.
- A person, usually out of touch with God, does not have the kind of self-knowledge which makes commitment possible and reliable.
- Wide sexual experience leads to marriage being interpreted as 'being tied down'.

These kinds of issues need to be faced wisely in early adulthood, so that they do not drag on through the relationships which follow including marriage.

Growth into marriage

What often strikes older married couples is the triviality of the concerns during the early development of a relationship towards marriage. There was this misunderstanding or that. There was a reticence about revealing this problem or that, when one point of marriage is to share problems. There was a concern about appearance, when now putting rollers in is a pleasant bedtime ritual. There were worries about status and money which are now swamped in gratitude to God for life. There was a concern for achievement, when now a good loving relationship is achievement enough, and actually it is the opposite of achievement, because it is from God. Dating and mating couples therefore need some perspective on their relationships which is less than immediate. Life needs to be seen in the context of God's purposes. What is really valuable in each one of us is not our IQ, dynamic personality, earning power or unstoppable sense of humour. Each of us and our partner are rich beyond our knowing in who we are before God. It is the quality of love, respect and faithfulness which will bring that out and create an enriching marriage. Friendship, dating and marriage are awesome processes as we meet and begin to know one another. They need to be treated with respect. There is a range of words like 'chaste', 'modest', 'pure' which actually help provide the conditions for heart to speak to heart.

Our culture is full of rushed relationships, skating over the surface of our personalities and often hurting with the friction. The deeper need and desire which we all have are for relationships, which because they are constructed on God's terms, allow us to open as person to person, to marry or not to marry.

6

COHABITATION

The meanings of the relationship

Cohabitation has surged as a recent form of intimate relationship in the modern West. Since the Reformation marriage has slowly become the norm, and living together was basically an underclass phenomenon, where the woman was seen as without respect. Bill Sykes and Nancy were Dickens' version in *Oliver Twist* and she finishes up murdered by the drunkard. There have been common law marriages, which although not formalised legally have been communally (and even legally) understood as marriage. Men have had mistresses, or paid prostitutes. There have been premarital and extra-marital affairs. But none of these is really equivalent to cohabitation, which has emerged over the last few decades as a common form of relationship for many couples. Like divorce it is common among urban, well-educated people and therefore looks like a modern trend. It also occurs throughout the West, although less in traditional Catholic countries. But 'it' may be too simple a word, for 'cohabitation' is a bit of a catch-all covering different kinds of relationship. In this chapter I will suggest that it has a number of meanings which are distinct and significantly so, and our main task is to work out what these are, and understand the character of the relationship which they entail.

There are a number of ways of defining cohabiting relationships, but perhaps the most straightforward is to look at them in terms of the ways they depart from marriage: *as living together in a sexual relationship without some of the patterns of commitment normally associated with marriage.* This will give us an understanding of what is missing from the relationship, and it will not differ significantly from the way the participants are likely to see it themselves, although, of course, cohabitants may vary in the way they view the relationship. Much of the sociological research uses quite crude categories which are easier to collect, but do not give much insight into the character of these relationships. Here we will try to identify what these different relationships mean and open up the dynamics which they involve.

With the kind of background we have already considered, the tendency of some couples to go for a form of cohabitation, rather than marriage, is readily understandable. The individualism, parental failure, fear of breakdown, distrust of the 'opposite' sex, and known levels of marital breakdown – all of these could lead couples not to want to define their relationship in terms of conventional marriage. This has happened. There are two overall groups – single cohabitees and separated and divorced ones (ST, 1995, 39). The scale of single cohabitation in Britain is difficult to establish accurately, but the proportion of women cohabiting with their future husband has risen from around 5 per cent in the mid-1960s to over 50 per cent now (ST, 1992, 46). Others are cohabiting and not marrying at all. After divorce or separation people seem highly likely to opt for cohabitation. In order to understand in more detail what may be going on in these relationships we now examine a number of semi-distinct forms.

Early temporary cohabitation

Here the pattern involves an understanding by one or both partners that the relationship involves no long-term commitment. Some situations, like being a student or working in a certain area, may be used as a time horizon for the relationship, or there may be a vague understanding that either person could move on if another relationship becomes more attractive. The seeming advantage is that the relationship offers a stable sexual partner and companionship, but without commitment or long-term ties.

However, this kind of relationship is often not planned or discussed before it is entered into (by 75 per cent in a survey by Macklin, see Buunk and van Driel, 1989, 7). After spending nights together, one partner may move in, perhaps keeping their own living quarters. The main reason for cohabitation is usually given as falling in love, but there is usually an understood limited commitment and degrees of independence. Children are not considered. Often education or career may be seen as a priority at this stage of life. Generally, the attitudes to sex are far from permissive; in the British national survey 70 per cent of cohabiting men and 80 per cent of women think that sex outside a live-in partnership is always or mostly wrong, although the figure drops to below a half for men with wider sexual experience (Wellings, 246–7, 258). Thus, the norm is often of going steady, although not always so (Ibid., 106). Here, therefore, we have young couples who enter a sexual relationship without defining its personal content.

What is going on here is difficult to discern. One argument is that some young women especially come from families with strained relationships, and the cohabiting may therefore be playing out needs for father hunger, family warmth or routes of escape (Buunk and van Driel, 1989, 56). Another view is that this relationship is *post-romantic* in that a couple will try out the process of being in love and sexual union, but without the belief that it can last. Reduced expectations are built into the relationship. It may reflect the idea that marriages seem not to work. There may also be economic pressure with one partner induced to move into the property of another – particularly younger women with older men. There are nearly twice as many women as men under twenty-five cohabiting and the difference is most marked with teenage girls (ST, 1994, 38). Another view is that the relationship reflects either the *New Wet Male* – the man who will not take on relationships with commitments, or the *Wary Woman* – who does not want to be lumbered with a useless or abusive man. What is likely, however, is that if one partner (it needs no more) sees this relationship as temporary, the relationship ends, perhaps with friendship, but often with hurt.

This is because the internal structure of the relationship poses a problem. On the one hand it often involves being in love, intimacy, full sexual experience of the partner and high levels of sharing. Each person must open up to the other person and respond to them. But the terms of the relationship are effectively uncommitted, short-term and independent. This is a recipe for hurt, disillusion and hardness. As a tutor a quarter of a century ago I can remember being confronted by two students madly in love who had decided to cohabit; within two months the two had parted with tears and some bitterness. The person you lived with has come along to the party, but with someone else. Often the break-up has an uneven impact; one pushes for greater commitment and the other backs off. Making love *is* effective commitment, but then it turns out not to be; the lie becomes evident. So even in intimacy people do not trust the other and are wary. Intimacy involves sharing our inmost character and feeling; this is not likely to happen when someone is likely to get off the bus at the next stop.

The live-in boyfriend

This model is older and more strongly associated with Black United States and Caribbean ethnic groups. It involves a family pattern in which the key is the relationship between mother and daughter. The daughter grows up and goes out to work. If she becomes pregnant, then it is the mother who takes on the primary role in bringing up the baby. The father of the new child may live in the home providing some financial support, but he may also move on, for the young mother is the primary source of income and the grandmother the primary carer. The family dynamics of this pattern are deep. Central is the pattern of trust and unconditional support between Mother and Daughter. Some sociologists think the pattern goes back to the era of slavery when the men were absent for long periods, were moved about and were given no respect. The men are marginalised, probably because they are likely to have no regular job or be transient workers, are not trustworthy in their sexual relationships and relate strongly to their own peer groups. Of necessity the male tends to be a *passive father*, who will be beset by a number of pitfalls like alcohol, drugs, gambling and criminality. This pattern is well known in the Caribbean and in the Black communities in the United States and Britain. Of course many Black marriages and families have a normal conjugal pattern, but the tenacity of this family pattern cannot be gainsaid. Black churches have fought this pattern by trying to give the father status and authority within the families of members. Yet levels of this kind of cohabitation have historically been substantially higher than for other ethnic groups.

But the pattern now has wider significance. White men growing up with restricted access to education, training and jobs are increasingly finding themselves without economic resources for marriage or access to housing. Young mothers, by contrast, may be given accommodation. In this situation younger men often become cohabitees or household visitors. In South Wales and other urban British areas, in Russia and Eastern Europe this kind of relationship is constantly becoming more common. Men's links with their children may be similarly shadowy, especially if Social Security spying is in operation. Essentially, the key element in this pattern is male economic impotence. It is poverty-driven.

But its dynamics are very destructive. Crucial is the position of the young Black male. Around adolescence he escapes from the often fearful control of his grandmother and mother. Maybe they will take him to church hoping he will turn out different. He escapes outside the home, with his peer group, and identifies with the adult men who represent the absent father. Normal educational and career routes are blocked and the focus is on sport, music, street credibility and sex. Because economic power is absent, some compensate by using physical power and violence in sexual and community relationships. Male self-respect is denied, when it should be centrally a question of our relationship with God who respects none of us especially and each of us in particular. The lack of social respect experienced by Black men has been allowed to be self-defining. They have often been *talked out* of their ability to provide love, faithful companionship, be a cherished husband and a good father by a destructive cultural pattern. It could be argued that there needs to be a fundamental religious transformation wherever this pattern is found so that God-given mutual respect and love can define marriages, replacing female power and disrespect and male assertiveness and transience.

The partial relationship

Another attitude is far more middle-class. It grows out of a career-orientated culture which has a number of acute pressures. Organisations run by middle-aged executives often pressure young people to very high levels of work and this spills into the rest of life. Career must come first for man and career woman. In addition, the guiding norm of the culture is individualism, freedom and independence. Often this relationship will be a highly articulate, carefully worked-out contract. Chris Barton shows an example.

- Absent truly extraordinary circumstances, we agree to spend at least one evening a week enjoying each other – alone together. An evening begins at 7 p.m.

- We will tell each other when we have sex with other people, and we will make an effort to communicate honestly about all other important relationships in our lives.
- Each of us will have individual control over the income we earn individually, in excess of that contributed to the fund for common expenses.
- We agree to stay together, absent intense pain, for four years or until our child is three years old, whichever is earlier (Barton, 1985, 63–68).

This idiom involves an invisible line running through the areas of life which are mutual and those which remain individual. Or to put it another way, some of the relationship is shared and other parts remain uncommitted. It is especially associated with a culture in which the young, upwardly-mobile work out what they are prepared to vest in a relationship and what they are not. The variations can be endless. Each partner may retain or share their own friends, career, capital resources, personal possessions, freedom and their ability to make independent choices. But again the model comes up against the reality of being human. We are whole people, created integral by God. Splitting is destructive and a source of internal stress. Sharing becomes hedged, unspontaneous. Calculations are complex. To share a bed, but not friends, soon becomes artificial. When one person changes job, what does this do to the relationship? Is the sexual relationship exclusive or not? As the relationship deepens, the partial limits become strained and the question is whether the relationship flows into other areas or remains channelled and restricted. Because a (marriage) union is meant to be whole, this artifice fragments either into marriage or into bargains between two individuals.

Here we have to face a grave structural weakness in the Western lifestyle. The present career demands on young employees, often drawing on the Japanese model of total loyalty to the company, are very heavy. Often profit-hungry executives are cutting the workforce and asking young employees to carry heavy loads. The hidden cost of this policy is that time which should be given to marital relationships and early child-rearing is not available. We now recognise that the economic costs of disrupted relationships and work burn-out which result from this run into billions. Many of these costs are created by channelling upwardly mobile young men and women into contractual cohabitation. 'Goodbye, my sweet. The Company is sending me to Japan. It's been nice knowing you.'

Trial marriage

Many people think of cohabitation as trial marriage, but it is important to establish what this means. Here there is an important distinction to make. Many couples decide to marry but then move in together before the wedding. This is not a trial, but is bringing forward the advent of the marriage without what may be seen as 'the formalities'. This is premarital cohabitation which we shall discuss later. Trial marriage is a *don't know* living together. We may marry or we may part. It is probably accepted by many people as acceptable, even advisable. Here again the idiom is different. The approach is pragmatic, to see if the lifestyle and process of living together works. Notice that 'it' works or does not. The idiom leaves the partners passive, almost as onlookers on the process, although other couples develop a more active orientation, saying that in cohabitation you have to make a relationship work and not rely on a bit of paper. Still, however, the question is whether he and she are committed to each other, not whether it works.

Here there are two serious problems. The first concerns the relationships which don't develop into marriage. In this situation one partner who has shared their life, body, emotions and hopes with the other is rejected. Nobody should face this kind of rejection. It is too deep and total.

Dating couples might not suit one another; that can be faced. But a person who has effectively given his/her love and body to the other is being dishonoured. We should not treat one another so. Sometimes, to avoid this outcome the withdrawing partner makes the relationship collapse, and it just peters out into a denial of what it earlier was. Whatever the outcome, it is tragic both for the rejected person and for the one who has hardened themselves to cut out. Handing over one's body on a sale or return basis is not good enough for marriage. The second problem is moving from passive to active. The question of whether the marriage will work or not is a different dimension from the wholehearted commitment of marriage. 'I love you' is a statement of the whole person. There is nothing behind it, nothing circumstantial; it is I who loves you. It is commitment, vow. There is power in this love. It draws on the way God has made us to live. When Paul says, 'For I am convinced that neither death nor life, neither angels nor demons, neither the present nor the future, nor any powers, neither height nor depth, nor anything else in all creation, will be able to separate us from the love of God that is in Christ Jesus' (Rom. 8:38–9), he is not saying 'I hope it works out'. Marriage is my choice, my commitment; it cannot be pragmatic, for each of our partners is worth more than that.

Premarital cohabitation

Many couples now live together *before* getting married. They have committed themselves to one another, and, the argument goes, why should we not live and sleep together now? Why wait? Or, we could say, if it is not the formality of the wedding service which makes a marriage, but the troth of one to the other, then cannot the marriage be constituted before the wedding? Obviously it can, and often is. But here the question arises as to why living together becomes especially urgent now, when it has not been so pressing in earlier times. The reason is because our view of time has changed. We demand the instant, including instant gratification. Relationships must blossom into fruition overnight. Yet marriage is likely to last forty or fifty years. The process of courtship is tender and involves stages of vulnerability. This other person should become known with sensitivity. They need to be allowed to make the choice of marriage (not of wedding) freely, without pressure or manipulation. The choice should also be a full personal one involving every aspect of life – feelings, past, friendships, family. A person enters Holy Matrimony; they enter wholly without reservation and they enter complete. All their decision-making processes have been brought together into the betrothal and marriage.

Premarital cohabitation then becomes like rushing up the building without bothering about the foundations. It loses the dignity and deliberation of chaste betrothal and marriage. It is rushed in a way which is likely to lead to doubts and regrets, rather than proceeding on a surety that 'for better, for worse' will work. The figures on marital breakdown after cohabitation suggest that the route from cohabitation to marriage, if it works out as such, is often not a good path of growth. There is therefore great wisdom in the process of chaste engagement or betrothal – the commitment to marry – followed by marriage, which involves the full giving of each to the other before God. What we have unlearnt is actually to our blessing.

Extra-marital cohabitation

Another group of people see cohabitation as a possibly longterm, mature relationship which they are content to live in without being married. They see cohabitation as replacing marriage or as a substantial prelude to marriage. This pattern is common in Scandinavia and a study by Wiersma suggests it is also present in the Netherlands as well as among other groups in most Western nations. It would be associated with educated, relatively affluent élites, and could be the strongest cultural trend around now. One question is whether this differs from marriage, although it is not called by that name. It could be *non-legal marriage*. Many couples living together either are already, or rapidly become, effectively married. They have a full, unconditional commitment to one another based on an understanding of live, faithfulness and companionship. They may feel that the legal piece of paper is irrelevant (as it is for those who are happily married in a normal legal sense). Indeed, the experience of many young people is that the legal piece of paper has not kept their parents together. What they want to rely on is the actual relationship. Fine. You can call it cohabitation, marriage or Stilton cheese, but if the relationship is a faithful union of love it is effective marriage. It is interesting that Paul in 1 Corinthians 7 focuses on the substance and not the formal quality of the relationship when addressing these issues. But the law should have a place. It should express the justice of the relationship, and one of the problems is the way the liberal definition of marriage law has led to it being vacuous and not much different. This is addressed in the chapter on law.

Second, many feel marriage is largely tied to the church, and because they have no Christian commitment, do not want to be married. Some have the view that the *church* blesses a wedding, and do not want it. This is a mistake. The crucial question is whether a marriage is formed in relation to God, by troth and commitment; the church merely witnesses to this bigger truth and reality. Sadly, the church focus on weddings rather than the ongoing reality of marriage has tended to obscure this fact. If a marriage is Christian in the full biblical sense it acknowledges the way love, faithfulness, the acknowledgement of sin and forgiveness must structure the relationship that develops. It is primarily a recognition of the unconditional truth of this love. My sadness is that so many people do not know what the Christian understanding of marriage is and what their commitment could be. For others this feeling may be tied to the expense and formality of weddings. Often they generate expenditure, involve social obligations and create tensions which many people would prefer to be without. But here, too, there are different levels of misunderstanding. Weddings can, of course, be very simple. The church should not be tied into status and performance, but only into good and pure relationships. There is nothing Christian about white wedding dresses.

Third, they may feel that 'it', being married, gets in the way of the actual relationship, and we could call this the *dynamic relationship* model. This is an interesting argument, although not one against marriage. If a couple relies on being married, a state which is behavioural and taken for granted, then problems can arise. In faithful marriage or cohabitation it is the actual love and trust in the relationship which count, and not having a ring on the finger. Here, cohabitees seem to face more problems. They are less likely to have stable relationships; there is more instability and thought of leaving the relationships, and they are less likely to be treated with respect and consideration. Thus the choice is not between a dynamic cohabiting relationship and being in a dead marriage, but between two kinds of relationship which stand or fall on their own terms. There may be other dynamics at work. Sometimes, a cohabiting partner runs to marriage when the relationship begins to look unstable. These are reactions, rather than the real thing.

Often this kind of cohabitation contains the understanding that things can change. It operates with pragmatic and changeable attitudes to relationships. If things don't go well, then there will be no legal wrangles and, if there are no children, it will be possible for a couple to walk away from one another. Sometimes, fatalism is a part of the approach. Either things work out or they do not. These attitudes mean that the partners have not really bonded to one another. Love is fierce, committed. It fights defeat, perseveres, suffers and learns.

There are three considerations which arise from this view

of cohabitation. Within it, deciding when unconditional commitment occurs may be more difficult, and surrounded by more fear and vulnerability than we have thus far recognised. Second, the legal protection of marriage is important in defining what is unjust in human relationships, and many cohabitees have been treated unjustly without any redress. Third, there is a central need for a couple to live in a relationship which is defined as love and trust to one another, as one lives *in* marriage. The integrity and honesty of the relationship will be revealed. Overall, this perspective misses out on what it meant to enter marriage. We enter a structure with norms which we obey. The truth of married love and union depends on God's faithfulness and love. Our response to God removes our autonomy. Christian marriage is therefore the truth which every cohabiting relationship needs. Without it, cohabitation is likely to be circumstantial and even destructive.

Post-marital cohabitation

Many people who are divorced or separated feel defeated by their earlier marriage. They may have been hurt and experienced a breakdown of trust. They may have lost faith in their own ability to form another permanent relationship, at least for a while. Often there are issues from the marriage which are still being sorted out. The solution often seems to be cohabitation, and it may include elements of the other patterns described above. However, there are two other dangers. If this relationship is in any sense a cause of the breakdown of the earlier relationship, it will be flawed, both in the wrong done to the earlier spouse and in tempting the transferring partner away from addressing what was wrong in the earlier relationship. The collusion may cost dear. The second danger is of the earlier problems occurring in the different, later relationship where they do not have any direct possibility of resolution.

There is another area here which must be acknowledged. Many cohabiting relationships do involve a deep sense of failure. Knowing that sex meant little more to the first partner than gratification is not affirming. Being rejected for another woman or man is heart-rending. Walking out on someone is not easy to live with. Deserting children who trusted you does not build self-respect. Having sex with people before you even know them does not generate good friendship. So we are not talking here about a triumphalist movement which is pointing the way to the future, as much as people who are acknowledging and facing defeat and failure. The Christian faith does not allow a bruised piece of grass to be broken or a smouldering candle to be snuffed out. Although marriage may be right, that is not the issue when people are suffering. The issue is why they are suffering.

Thus, cohabitation, except where it is effectively marriage, may contain many more problems than has sometimes been recognised. Partial trust, temporary commitment and 'try it and see' relationships do not really work in this intimate bond where self-giving, trust and permanence are central to the joy and excitement of the relationship. Sadly, cohabitation may come to be seen as another stage in the destructive outworking of individualism in the lives of many who never really know the security and complete trust which should be the hot core of their partnership. And for those who are *really* married, it seems a pity to walk up the aisle backwards.

7

FAITH AND MARRIAGE

The universal Christian understanding of marriage

The understanding of marriage thus far is of a universal institution which is God-given and to be understood in terms of biblical revelation. This raises a number of issues which will be tackled in this chapter. Some are of a general conceptual character and others concern the actual meaning and dynamics of marriage in relation to people's faith. First there is the question of whether an understanding of marriage can be universal and Christian at the same time. Is this possible? The answer is, yes, if it is true. Then it supplies a universal understanding of this part of the human condition whether people acknowledge it directly or not, and it is better that people do acknowledge it. The Bible gives us an acute awareness of cultural variations which are pathological, because human sin is built into structures, attitudes and human social perspectives. Thus, establishing good marriages, seen in the right way, is a continual fight in human culture. It is not an automatic process, but requires people to form and live with a proper understanding of marriage.

This is not conformity to a particular cultural model. It allows considerable cultural diversity. A Greek husband fetching the ice may well be showing love which an Eskimo husband would not be. The crucial dynamic here is the awareness that many, indeed all, cultures are open to critical evaluation because they are playing out of tune with God's music for marriage. The standard is God's, not self-created human ones.

This raises the question of the relationship between those who do not acknowledge Christianity and this Christian understanding of marriage. The primary conclusion is that it does matter, fundamentally, whether people and married couples respond to God and the Judaeo-Christian revelation or not. This is because the central route to human self-knowledge is to relate and listen to the God who has made us. Not having this relationship in place is to set everything awry. Acknowledging God and living obediently in Christian marriage are the route of human blessing, because they involve living in accordance with the way we are created and intended to live. Those who shape their lives by other faiths or philosophies also shape their marriages in the same way. Romantic love, a contractual view, individualism, a central drive for sex are really the motors running their lives and marriages. Thus the choice of going for a Christian marriage or not is a central one.

This also gives us an understanding of the relationship between the marriage of Christians and Christian marriage. The latter is not the former. Christians who marry have access to God's love and faithfulness. They can live substantially in the fullness of the biblical truths of marriage or they can in part ignore them or allow them to be swamped by other faiths and cultural impulses. Exactly the same battles for Christian marital formation which Paul was facing in ancient Corinth are being waged in other cultures within the marriages of Christians now. Some married Christians are substantially pagan, individualist, traditional, family-centred or moralist in the way they live their married lives. One of the main aims of this study is to allow Christians to enter more fully into Christian marriage and to show how central the Christian faith is to marriage.

Marriage in different faiths and cultures

In many parts of the world traditional religions generated a family-centred view of marriage which contained marriage within rites and patterns of deference which were strongly enforced over centuries. In Japan the Shinto rites of community life and the Buddhist household ones made marriage a pattern which happened within tight patterns of family deference and the assumption of male dominance and honour (Hendry). Now this pattern has been met by a tide of Western relational views and by acute financial and housing pressures which are creating nuclear units surfing off into new ways of living and consuming. In China the traditional, male-dominated Confucian family was overturned by Mao and the law requiring family size to be limited to one child is undermining the possibility of any family-centred view. This is an amazing reversal of traditional Chinese family culture, and we do not know where it will lead, although marriage will become more central. In India the traditional family is still very powerful, partly because it still functions overwhelmingly as the economic unit of organisation. Hindu views of family contain marriage within a firm patriarchal model. Some traditions emphasise a total identification of the woman with her man, as with the ancient practice of *suttee*, where the wife threw herself on her husband's funeral pyre, but this is atypical. Much stronger is a dualism; men run society, the economy, politics and religion, while the wife and mother runs the home. She is a goddess who firmly controls her own domain. Indeed, the significance of male and female deities runs quite deep, in that they represent quite ultimate polarisations of gender. His world and her world contend religiously. Again, however, Indian marital culture had been transformed by the idiom of romantic love, conveyed by an overwhelming explosion of film, music and art. Arranged marriages operating within a concept of duty and family order now vie with romantic liaisons which push the Hollywood idiom to the limit. This takes place alongside views in Hinduism and especially Buddhism which see the woman as a dangerous temptress (Paul). The cultural transformation which is resulting is vast and its outcome unpredictable.

In Africa a similar pattern has emerged. Traditional marriage was usually patriarchal, male-dominated and contained within family and tribal patterns. It is possible to idealise this pattern, but it was often characterised by polygamy, superstition, arranged marriages, male violence and a considerable degree of male laziness based on using the work of women. In West Africa, however, some women had a high degree of independence based on trade, business and a reconstructed family life. This pattern was disturbed by Christian missionary activity and the insistence on monogamy in the church. Monogamous, faithful marriage has now become the norm among many cultures in sub-Saharan Africa, but not without problems. Churches often insisted on divorce for all but one wife on conversion. There also emerged a pattern of 'church wife' – the high status proper wife – and other concubines and liaisons, or 'inside wives' and 'outside wives' (Parkin and Nyamwaya, 1981, 247–61). As the second wife says, 'Sarah! What Sarah are you telling me? Do you have someone in the dark! So you came to let me know about it just in time so that I may understand that I have become the third in line?' (Buule, 1875, 7). Christian marriage therefore competes with other traditional forms in many cultures. However, Westernism also now has a deep impact on African marriage. Cohabitation, gender conflict, migrant labour, prostitution and divorce are common. Thus, here the three views, traditionalist, Christian and Western vie for cultural weight.

Islamic views of family and marriage partly derive from Judaic and Christian roots – there is prohibition of adultery – but it also reflects a series of different emphases. Marriage is seen as a duty and act of obedience to Allah, and is more or less obligatory; singleness by contrast is seen as a defective. Men are seen as the protectors and maintainers of women, because Allah has given them more strength, and the wife is expected to be obedient to the husband. The principle of *hijab* – seclusion – or the limitation of the woman to the home and behind the veil is one that has shaped the Islamic view of marriage deeply. This is a tremendous issue throughout Islamic countries, because it has produced a strong patriarchal pattern which is heavily institutionalised. The Prophet sanctioned light wife-beating for women who contravened the teaching of the Qur'an, and male violence is sometimes a serious problem. This attitude is now meeting Western attitudes much more deeply influenced by mutuality and a feminism is emerging which looks set to generate a difficult cultural conflict. Polygamy was permitted, although on a very slight Qur'anic reference – up to four wives, but this has been restricted or prohibited in a number of Islamic countries. Divorce is strongly condemned by Muhammad, 'Of all things which have been permitted, divorce is the most hated by Allah', but it is allowed. In some Islamic traditions the discretion of divorce has been granted to the husband, as compared with much more restrictive legal control on the wife. This too generates tensions. Much of the emphasis in Islam is towards good family and marital behaviour in accordance with the Shari'ah, but the centrality of the male as protector and maintainer of the woman raises a structural issue which many Islamic marriages are having to address (I Doi, 1984; Bashier, 1985; Mernissi, 1991). Young migrant members of Islamic families face issues in Western culture which jar with the traditional concepts and rapid change is likely in their views of marriage.

This ferment of change worldwide requires the answers to some fundamental questions about the relation of family and marriage, the nature of marriage, but especially about the inner character of the relationship between man and woman which constitutes marriage. The tendency is for family-centred views of marriage to be challenged, and male power is at least challenged. But overall there is a tremendous dynamic for change, which really focuses on the nature of marriage. Here the models on offer are Westernism in its romantic and individualist versions and Christianity, and it is this that we now consider.

The inner meaning of marriage.

Marriage must be seen in terms of a faith, religion or world view. It is culturally shaped by a perspective on the whole of life, and broadly those now on offer are a Judaeo-Christian creational world view, or one which puts humanity at the centre of life's meaning. Seeing marriage in terms of the Christian faith means calling on the insights of faith to perceive the relationship with greater depth and awareness. There are many biblical truths which locate and form our cultural responses to marriage. We are created *persons* before God and should know the integrity of our own personhood, and that of our spouse, as children of God. We should know our wholeness before God. We are called to love the Lord our God with all our heart, soul, mind and strength and we should therefore know and grow into a *wholehearted* love of our spouse. We should know the strength of the union of marriage as two people coming together. Coming to know this one person fully is more than a lifetime task. All aspects of life should be shared, and shared under the norm of love which is patient, kind and sacrificial. The love union of Christian marriage, as presented in Chapter 3, therefore involves insights into the meaning of marriage which should be universal. This is what the relationship is meant to be like. The potential quality of this union goes beyond where we are now; it is a matter of faith and open commitment before God. It is a continual pilgrimage.

Adopting this perspective on marriage is a choice. The Bible presents us with an understanding of ourself and our partner which is life-transforming, a faith. The other main contender in our culture is *individualism*. It begins with a belief in *self-knowledge* and is *self-referential*. Religiously and relationally the partner is an outsider to this faith. It presumes that 'I know myself, and the problem is that other people do not understand me.' This agenda stifles growth and self-awareness, and sets up the idea that 'My partner does not understand me.' The truth is different. God's knowledge of us is complete. Psalm 139 sets out how God has searched us and known us. We are totally known by our Creator, and such knowledge is too comprehensive for us. Our self-knowledge is very limited and often mistaken. It takes most of us the rest of our lives to understand what really happened in our upbringing, and our knowledge continually lags behind our experiences. Our capacity for illusion seems endless. We could say, being simplistic, that our self-knowledge seldom reaches 30 per cent. Our friends may know 10 per cent, if we are lucky. Our spouse may know 25 per cent, or even an infuriating 31 per cent, but the deepest truth of marriage is that a couple is growing towards self-knowledge and knowledge of the spouse before God. In Paul's unforgettable words, set out in the context of showing the centrality of love, 'Now we see but a poor reflection; then we shall see face to face. Now I know in part; then I shall know fully, even as I am fully known' (1 Cor. 13:12). Our hope therefore lies, not in our self-knowledge, but in God's knowledge of us, personal and mutual, into which we may grow, and this is the reality in which marriage is best nurtured. Individualism, the worship of my ego, as the central meaning of life, is a lie.

Sin in marriage

Alongside this opening up of who we are and what the nature of relationships is, the Christian faith presents us with a diagnosis of problems. The current individualist culture tends to say that individuals are OK, and when there are problems, the marriage is at fault and should probably be terminated. Thus, for this culture the institution of marriage is seen to be problematic. The biblical understanding is far more probing and does not accept the patterns of self-pleading and self-justification which our culture is generating. A man blames his marriage for his adultery; a driver blames his car for going through the red light. There is no person who has effectively caused a divorce who is not on the run from self-knowledge. The biblical analysis of sin, personal, mutual, cultural stays with what is really wrong with us. It refuses the illusions. Often it is painful, but it does not lie. The healing comes through open wounds and gentle surgery.

Thus, marriage remains the route to self-knowledge, perhaps one of the greatest, but the marriage of Christians is subject to diagnosis with love – no anaesthetic, but love.

Christianity also does not allow a relationship to disintegrate to blame, possibly the most destructive form of marital relating. Blame is what one partner does to another on the basis of a supposed or actual wrong. It has been evident in marital relationships since Eden: 'The woman you put here with me – she gave me the fruit of the tree, and I ate it.' Blame is ruled out at a number of levels. First, it involves one partner in judging and condemning the other, when only God is judge. Second, it usually requires a construction of reality which is partial, incomplete and motivated by self-righteousness. Any good counsellor insists on hearing both, or many, sides of a story, especially when there is recrimination, because one story is likely to misrepresent, exonerate and dump guilt. Blame in marriage without an awareness of one's own failures is simply inaccurate. Third, blame cuts out the human response of recognition and repentance. A person should always, without a hard heart, be able to come to a recognition of culpability and repent. Fourth, the recognition of sin is primarily before God through the gentle power of the Holy Spirit to convict and reveal judgement, not through the judgement of others. So whatever is wrong in a marriage finds its central meaning and truth before

God, not in relation to a partner and his/her blame. It was after David had sinned by committing murder and adultery with Bathsheba that he penned,

> For I know my transgressions,
> and my sin is ever before me.
> Against You, You only have I sinned
> and done what is evil in your sight,
> so that you are proved right when you speak
> and justified when you judge.
>
> (Ps. 51:3–4)

It is this realism which needs to filter down into the arrogance of many of our relationships. 'A broken and contrite heart, O God, you will not despise' (Ps. 51:17).

Knowing the truth and throwing out the rubbish

The Christian Good News is that we are not lost in any of our failures. The lostness is often the sense that there is no way we can construct of ourselves anything better. And this is true. Total depravity in Calvin's sense does grasp our whole lives. Sin spreads and infects, because we are whole people. Similarly, because marriage does not allow in principle compartmentalisation, a problem in marriage cannot be boxed. Many of us try to compartmentalise sin – pornography, drinking, sexual relationships, materialism, bad temper are, we think, put in a box. But it does not work. If you are materialist at work, you will be so at home. Thus, of ourselves we are lost in our failures and many struggling couples are aware of this. There is no health in our relationship. It has all gone wrong. There are no bootstraps. The solution is beyond our *doing*.

But we have God's help. Not just as a new agenda. Or as diagnosis. Or as sympathy. God with us was not just a form of divine empathy, but the Son of God with us. The sins which rack our lives – pride, arrogance, aggression, lust, self-opinion, revenge, hatred, status-seeking were experienced by Jesus as victim, but not as perpetrator. 'He was led like a lamb to the slaughter, and as a sheep before her shearers is silent, so he did not open his mouth' (Isa. 53:7). That he who did no sin should suffer for our human sins, is the most outrageous human act. It reflects the murder of innocents still going on each week of our history through war. But our lie is God's truth. That Jesus should suffer and die on the cross for our sins, that God is with us to that extent, is an expression of love beyond desert or our understanding. It is grace. It is Christ bearing our sins in his body on the cross. It is atonement. This is often poisonously misunderstood. Christ's atonement is no God-required blood ritual. *Human-kind*, in the form of the Romans and Jews, were the perpetrators of the suffering and death. They produced the blood as human sin and evil has throughout all centuries and in all cultures. The love of God is to have received the suffering and death, to willingly be made sin for us. The anger and hatred which Christ experienced and exposed: 'You are trying to kill me' led him willingly and with open eyes to the cross and death. The sin was carried, not on human terms, but on God's terms, directly, personally, fully, by death. The depth of God's help and the astonishing terms of it are beyond our ways of thinking. We are rescued from sin, reconciled by forgiveness with God and one another, made just when engulfed in injustice, bathed in love and grace of God and introduced to the resurrection power of God. This help does not come from our past, circumstances, or the experience of a sinful and unjust world, but from the self-giving love of God in the face of human evil. Because the terms of life are God-given – we in spite of our powers are mere creatures – the terms of life in Christ rule. God's love, grace and forgiveness do rule human affairs. 'This is how we know what love is: Jesus Christ laid down his life for us ... We love because he first loved us' (1 John 3:16, 4:19).

This is fundamentally true of marriage. The humanistic temptation is to draw conclusions about ourselves and our partners which are ego-referenced or experiental. If those conclusions take our own sinfulness as the last word, if they stop with selfishness, hardheartedness and lack of awareness, then we miss out on the truths which are deeper than ourselves seen in our own terms, but are the fundamental truth about ourselves in relation to God. John, who walked about with Jesus, touched and talked with him, knew this better than anyone.

If we claim to be without sin, we deceive ourselves and the truth is not in us. If we confess our sins, he is faithful and just and will forgive us our sins and purify us from all unrighteousness ... This then is how we know that we belong to the truth, and how we set our hearts at rest in his presence whenever our hearts condemn us. For God is greater than our hearts, and he knows everything. (1 John 2:8–9, 3:19)

Thus, the truth is often greater, and more full of love and joy, than we directly experience or even suspect. Marital salvation is locked into the suffering, victorious love of God. All of us can always look to Jesus and love our partner.

The Christian wedding

The traditional expression of Christian marriage is a church wedding. It is possible to mythologise a wedding, to try to make it something in itself, an event, magic, the experience of a lifetime or even a central religious sacrament. It is not. It is just the start of a marriage. But what kind of marriage? Now it is time to suggest why a Christian wedding is the proper start to a marriage. First, the wedding is fully personal (whole and Holy Matrimony). It is not sex first, or any other ragged development of commitment, but here each to the other gathers all that they are and gives unreservedly. Second, it brings together different aspects of the relationship – the shared faith, the legal structure, the friends and community, the families, the personal history of the couple and their feelings for one another in this unique event before God. Third, it is a vow before God which acknowledges the centrality of the relationship with God in life and marriage. Marriage is entered into on God's terms of love, faithfulness and forgiveness, and from a living faith. These are stated – 'forsaking all other ... for better, for worse, for richer, for poorer, in sickness and in health, as long as we both shall live'. The point, therefore, is not to 'have a wedding', but to live a marriage in this kind of way. A wedding does not have to be white, expensive, in church, drowned in food and drink or an act of social display.

It should be the beginning of a life of blessing together with God.

8

SEX AND MARRIAGE

Our bodies and God

We are all given our bodies; we do not earn them or achieve them. They are one of the great gifts of life and exhibit the glory of the Creator, from the hairs on our head to the balance in our toes and ears. We have awesome bodies. We *are* bodies; this is the way God has created us. They express our different personhood – face, colour, size, bone structure, yet we are all roughly the same. Even the differences between men and women can be culturally exaggerated. The giveness of who we, and others, are bodily is almost taken for granted. Why should we be self-conscious about it? It is the way life is. Most of the time we walk, eat, rest and think on that basis. But behind the taken for granted-ness should be an awe that we are God's crafting, and we bodily stand in open relationship with God. Paul expressed it by saying, 'We are a temple of the Holy Spirit.' This sense of the bodily integrity of each person, and their glory before God, should be one of the central truths of life for all people. Those who lose it because of physical or sexual attacks, or social comparisons, should be angry because they have been deprived by other people of the truth of their identity before God, and they should bodily know the truth of who they are before God rather than degrade their lives on what others have done to or think about them. That is the meaning of holiness.

This central principle involves bodily care. The history of this process is often overlooked, but Shorter and others have opened it up. What is so wonderfully made (the frontiers of medical science continually open up new land-scapes of design) should be respected. This is why drugs, tobacco, alcohol, stimulants and other body addictions are wrong; they are like taking a sledgehammer to a Rembrandt. Respect for the body must remain through eating, illness, handicap and even death. Cultural forces like ideas of beauty often distort it, even to the extent of generating anorexia (Freedman, 1988, Crowley and Himmelweit, 1992, 90–109). Our social intercourse should therefore respect one another's bodies; violence, scorn, abuse, junk food, bodily mutilation all involve disrespect.

There are two distortions of bodily integrity before God. The first is the widespread extent of body status. We can see this from the well-attested fact that people who are tall tend to get top and probably better jobs. There is an incredible status system which revolved around height-based superior-ity or inferiority – a sheer nonsense. But body status has spread. There are vast industries making money by inviting people to see their bodies as better than those of others – fashion, cosmetics, slimming, much of the health and fitness industry have as their aim enhancing people's sense of self-worth by comparison with others. Body status is attached to all kinds of physical conditions like having blonde hair, a big mouth, bulging biceps, being tall or whatever. The industries promoting these ideals produce three results. First, anyone who relies on their broad shoulders or big bosom has lost the full sense of their identity before God, and they are enslaved by that on which they rely. Second, people are trained to treat others as inferior, and many others feel inferior. In fact, *most* others feel inferior. The anorexic feels fat, the fashion-conscious person regularly feels badly dressed, and the person with tinted hair sees every grey hair. Third, there is often something grotesque when the fully developed form of body status appears – the total cosmetic woman, the all-muscle man or the beanpole slimmer. These distortions should point back to the biblical truth of the equal-given integrity of all bodies before God. When we are content with who we are as bodies, then we will be able to live together without the covert hostility of body status and a cultural sense of bodily inadequacy.

This is also reflected in our view of beauty. Everybody wants to marry someone who is beautiful, and by and large everybody has. God has created all of us beautiful – every child, every face in the carriage of the London Underground. As a portrait painter I cannot understand how women want to obscure the delicacy and sensitivity of their faces by cosmetics. Many others of us obscure our beauty by worry, anger, overeating and lack of sleep. This created beauty of our faces and bodies is, of course, not uniform. We are all very different and it is the richness of created beauty that we actually explore throughout our lives and in our spouses. Yet many culturally created idioms of beauty exercise extreme tyranny over our thought. Fat African men (and some American males) are seen as beautiful. Other men must be thin. Blonde, black, red or brown hair is seen as beautiful, when actually all are. Fashions change arbitrarily each year, and age is either beautiful or a disaster. Most of these judgements are so arbitrary, and so strongly based on sales empires, that one wonders why anybody is taken in by these manufactured idioms of beauty. Yet they have many of us in thrall.

Does sex exist?

Many readers will be quite annoyed by now. They have turned to the chapter on sex first, because their culture has taught them that this is how to read, and then found that it ignores the subject. And now they face the headline, Does sex exist? But it is a question worth asking. As a word and dominant idea with its current meaning it is remarkably recent, entering popular usage well since World War II (Copley, 1989, 198–227; Weeks, 1981). The problem is this. 'Sex' is 'it'; it is an activity domain or what people 'have'. It has been divorced in many people's consciousness from questions of personality, truth, body and the nature of relationships. Giddens calls it *plastic sex*. Sometimes it is portrayed as a basic human need, like water or defecation. Actually, of course, 'it' (using the idiom) is not like that at all. Children and many adults are not sexually conscious. Friends, work colleagues, traffic wardens and even milkmen do not 'need' sex in their daily relationships. The 'it' is largely a creation of a number of tawdry and cheapening industries – prostitution, sex-pushing magazines and newspapers, films and books – which have pushed consumer sex as a way of making big profits out of the gullibility of people. Perhaps the Emperor had his clothes on all the time. There is the possibility, therefore, that 'sex' is a big myth created by these industries since 1945 while really 'it' does not exist at all. God exists; bodies exist and persons exist, but does 'sex'?

Our answer to this question needs to be a bit more rigorous. Sexual activity obviously exists, *but in the context of a personal relationship within which it has its meaning*. If this is the case, 'it' cannot be separated from that meaning. Some sexual activity, it is true, does take place outside a real relationship – induced by a woman's picture or masturbation. Most people would see this kind as defective in some way, mainly because it is using physical sensations in a self-gratificatory way. Here we see the hinge around which a Christian understanding of sex emerges. Sex which has *the self* as its meaning and goal is wrongly seen, because sexual activity is meant to be relational. The Bible calls this false view 'lust', and identifies it as the source of a whole range of evils to which all of us are open either as actors or victims. This self-gratificatory meaning is pushed strongly by our culture. 'It' allows sexual activity to be reified as a thing-in-itself. 'It' generates rape, sexual abuse, unloving sexual contact, fear of being used, prostitution and pornography, and 'it' is also undermining many marriages, because of the dynamics which this self-gratificatory view sets underway.

Thus, we conclude that 'sex' does exist, but in a degenerate form of relationship which corresponds more to the biblical meaning of lust. Otherwise sexual activity is best seen within the context of the relationships which give them meanings. 'Sex' largely does not exist, except as a pathology which damages those who espouse it.

Sexual rubbish in marriage

There are a number of areas where couples carry sexual rubbish into their marriage. Many grow from the idea of 'it'. If self-gratification has been a primary motivation for marriage, then one or both partners will tend to feel used and violated in their bodies. There is irony in Paul's comment, 'It is better to marry than to burn with passion' (1 Cor. 7:9) for this motive for marriage dishonours the person. Most sexologists would confirm that the ego-focus of gratification leads to a rushed, aggressive, violent and dominant sexual relationship which spoils the mutuality of love. To enjoy the God-given relationship the focus needs to be on giving and receiving one another, not on needs and drives. This mutuality is summed up in a key verse in the Song of Solomon 'Do not arouse or awaken love until it so desires' (S. of S. 2:5).

Another set of problems arise from previous sexual relationships, which are a common experience for many Western young people. The effects of these are various and not fully understood, but they include the following. Sometimes earlier relationships will have been seen just in terms of experience and gratification; then the tendency will be to bring a hardened, even technical, attitude to lovemaking. The partner may well fear, 'Will I be any different from the others?' At other times the earlier relationships will have involved some commitment, possibly deep. Here there are a variety of possible problems. There may well be grieving and sense of loss from these relationships, or guilt at the rejection which they involved. If this is not faced, there is merely a hardening of heart. Moreover, sexual giving loses its sense of wholeheartedness; sexual history makes this less than the complete giving which marriage is meant to be. There may be a temptation to compare partners, and a sense of sexual fidelity and trust will need to be constructed, rather than being an automatic part of the relationship. Reactions, possibly inappropriate, from the previous relationship, will feed into the marriage. At present there is an obvious inconsistency in young people's responses. On the one hand, sexual relationships before marriage are seen as acceptable, but faithfulness in marriage or a steady relationship is largely seen as normative. As the recent movement towards teenage chastity attests, faithfulness is best seen as a lifelong commitment. Earlier sexual experience can translate into marital adultery, because it encourages a shallow view of the sanctity of relationships. Rather than previous sexual experience being treated as inconsequential (for it is not), it needs to be faced, if necessary with remorse, so that there is a real sense of marital sexual sanctity.

Patterns of sexual addiction related to pornography and other sexual cultures can spoil a relationship by creating expectations and pressures which control the relationship as well as dishonouring the partner. Again the underlying dynamic is wrong. Doing 'it', or having such an experience, dominates the interpersonal relationship and undermines the freedom of both partners to express what they really feel in the relationship. A good sexual relationship in marriage has to be based on the honest expression of what each partner feels. If there is no feeling of love, then it should not be bodily expressed, because the end result is a sense of emptiness and hypocrisy.

Also significant, however, is the extent to which parental attitudes to sexuality may have shaped the next generation. These can take a variety of important forms. 'Men are all bastards and can't be trusted' should be wrong, whatever the mother's experience. Some fathers convey that older wives are sexually unattractive. The use of threats and manipulation by parents will induce fear, even if children are not directly involved. Lack of bodily respect and faithfulness to the other, or an absence of self-respect for the body and the right to marital faithfulness may be passed on. Often sexuality can be narrowly defined as 'looking pretty' or 'being macho' by parents who collude in bringing up children the same way. But the level of marital breakdown and parental adultery in many Western marriages must mean that many marriage relationships, however much immediate joy there is, must start with a lack of confidence. There is a generation of parents whose attitudes to sex their children need to substantially repudiate. Actually, whatever the problems created by parents it is quite possible to throw out the rubbish and establish the sexual integrity and purity of a marriage for life.

The biblical doctrine of marital sexual relations

Marriage is a lifelong union of two persons in love. It is an unqualified commitment. The love is not optional. It is God's command that husbands and wives love one another and each person commits her or himself in troth (in truth) and by vow in Christian marriage to that commitment. The union is a full act and process of self-giving, and of receiving the other person. As we have emphasised, this union is not an external contract, but an unconditional bonding in which each receives all of the other. Fully coming to know the other person will take sixty or more years, but it is also realised in principle from the beginning of the marriage. With the marriage each partner gives, also, his or her body to the other. This act is important. It can be done because the bond of unconditional trust is there. But it is also tremendous, because the created integrity and ownership of our own bodies before God which each of us has as a basic right and condition of life are at this point handed over to another. This requires trust and it should be marked by respect and joy. Paul makes clear the equality and reciprocal character of this body giving. 'The wife's body does not belong to her alone, but also to her husband. In the same way, the husband's body does not belong to him alone but also to his wife' (1 Cor. 7:4). This is a remarkable, but powerful statement; it emphasises the two-way mutual giving of bodies/selves which marriage is as something which is devoid of fear and reserve. The sexual joy of marriage is thus in the free giving and receiving of body love. If there is no love, then the pleasure will be unreal. It can only properly be done with one person within marriage. Another sexual relationship, as many have discovered, necessarily involves giving up the possibility of this trust and openness.

We thus move to the heart of marital sex. Marital sex works on a scale which few sociologists have recognised because it is so normal (Gardella). It works because it is a true expression of a faithful relationship. The statement made by the bodies is true, it is an expression of love which is meant and is permanent. This is why marriage is universal; there is no other possibility of a sexual relationship with full integrity. Cohabitation says it might work. Casual sex that this is a passing phase. An affair is a bit risky. *But marital sex is a true expression by the bodies of husband and wife of unconditional love and personal giving*. When there is complete trust, there is also the complete freedom of bodily sharing.

Although we have temporarily moved to the 'it' language, the frame of reference is different. Married couples share their bodies with one another. This normally means sexual arousal when intimate, unclothed bodies come together; the Creator has so designed us. But the meaning is shared *bodies* for life in work, food, exercise, rest and play. Indeed, it is now becoming clear that bodies are more important than sex, than the 'it'. We share our bodies in sickness and health. They reflect the experience and problems of life. They declare a person's glory and what is happening in a marriage. They carry early family experiences. Bodies in marriage can reflect a variety of problems – self-obsession, lack of self-acceptance, stress, aggression and a need for conformity. What they should reflect is tenderness, respect and self-giving, a process whereby each body is cherished by the other and given freely from the heart. Gentle body cherishing is the only sexual technique.

The central sexual issue in every marriage is thus not technique, but sharing bodies in love. Most sexual problems arise when life does not express love and 'sex' is expected to. If the wife feels, 'All he wants is sex', implying that the rest of life is without love and care, then bed will be marked by resentment. It is the consistency of day-to-day love and personal enjoyment of one another which shapes the meaning of what is expressed physically. This is because being loved is more important than 'having sex'. It is interesting that now with widespread knowledge of sexual techniques available to married couples, we have marriages breaking down on a massive scale, when earlier they were not. Actually, the techniques do not matter. If you are married for forty or fifty years you get to know one another physically quite well. The real issue is whether a couple loves one another. That is the central issue of desire.

Adultery

Over the last few decades there has been a process of justifying adultery which has gone on in the media and in many people's minds. There is a variety of arguments. Sometimes, it is 'having a little bit on the side'. This view trivialises the activity and sees it as of no consequence. At the same time, of course, it trivialises the person's sexual activity with their wife or husband. The person used in this process is cheapened as well as the spouse. Another slant is to justify adultery through 'falling in love'. Hollywood has been conveying this idiom for years. There are repeated patterns here. In some marriages one partner, say the wife, has been doing most of the work, while the other partner becomes increasingly self-indulgent. This self-indulgence, and possibly guilt, lead him to opt out into adultery. Rather than being a process of 'falling in love', it is actually an expression of increased selfishness. Many other examples of 'falling in love' are an expression of pride – 'I'm still attractive', 'I'm too good for her' or 'Why doesn't she realise how wonderful I am?' Others are sheer escapism. The person is blindly 'in love', when actually they are on the run from unsolved problems and attitudes which they (usually) have generated in the marriage. The husband who states to a woman at work that his wife does not understand him is precisely wrong. She does understand him and the problem is what she understands only too well, but he cannot see that. Others are just caught up in a culture of promiscuity and deception which undermines their marriage anyway. What is evident is the lack of self-knowledge revealed by those involved in adultery. There is a self-indulgent stupidity involved in the process of deciding that it is OK to 'have extramarital sex'.

It is, of course, always disastrous. It is dishonouring a wife or husband, and using another person to do so. It is bodily undermining the truth of marriage, and is therefore an effective expression of divorce, and is recognised as such by Jesus (Matt. 19:9). It is an absolute prohibition in the Ten Commandments and should never happen. Those who participate in it dishonour and wrong the partner to whom they are unfaithful and themselves. There are frequently lies about a 'marriage really being over' which has been fatally undermined by adultery. It is never merely a symptom, but always is an act against the spouse and the marriage.

The cultural change

At present there is a massive cultural battle. Generations coming into marriage are wrongly taught that having multiple sexual partners does not matter, and that sex is some kind of required personal therapy. Industries of promiscuous sex wash over them. At the same time they experience a lack of body integrity and are taught egocentric and impersonal attitudes towards sex. Sex is surrounded by mistrust and lack of personal respect. What suffers is the intimacy and trust of marriage where a couple can know one another without reserve and with joy. The fight to redeem relationships into joyful and good experiences of love and faithfulness involves changing a cultural tide; it is time we started.

9

MARRIAGE AND PERSONS

Personhood and marriage

For many people marriage is a shock. Often, this is because of what they find out about themselves. Previously, they were easy-going, tolerant and broad-minded, but now they insist on idiosyncrasies which are obviously arbitrary, or display attitudes which have no obvious source. What is going on here? It is not difficult to see the dynamic of this process. Intimacy and closeness bring self-revelation. The powerful processes by which many of us cut ourselves off from exposure are broken down by marriage. This is so good for many of us, but it should be good in the right way. Exposure and self-revelation depend on trust. Facing the truth about ourselves with pride and obstinacy is traumatic. Being put in a position where we learn a great deal about ourselves and refusing to learn is tragic. Every marriage therefore contains two personal journeys which are in union and which are full of the drama of self-revelation. Centrally we are all known by God and through God grow into self-knowledge, but for many of us the chief teaching aid is our husband or wife.

In this chapter we shall try to chart some of the central lessons that we need to learn in marriage about ourselves as persons. The starting-point and the end of the road, what we take with us into death, is our relationship with God, our Father. Whether in or out of marriage our relationship with God is who we are. God has made us and we did not make ourselves and our response of faith is the core, the heart of our lives. Love comes from God and it is God's love which

must shape us as persons and in marriage. There is no other
reliable way to live.

Personal freedom

Each of us as persons has freedom in the way we relate to
others. But this freedom needs to be understood in three
key ways. Many people, for example, feel trapped in marriage and other relationships. This is often because the terms
of these relationships are wrong; they may involve conformity, manipulation, domination or dependence. If we are to
be free from these forms of intimate oppression, the answer
is not to run from them, although some often do this, but to
face up to what is going on in them. In a word they can be
summarised by saying that the problem consists in one
person trying to live another person's life. This is actually a
stupid attitude, because each of us has been given one life
which is designed as a full-time occupation, and we can
therefore only live our own lives. But many of us are
convinced that if we can control the lives of those around
us, then *our* lives will work out. We try to make others love
us, look after us, give in to us or agree with us, or we suffer
this process. The truth is that each of us lives our own life
before God, and none of us should try to take over the lives
of others. It actually does not work. Domination breeds
resentment. Manipulation means that there is no real shared
purpose and induced dependence destroys the character of
the one with whom we share life. Jesus never controlled; it
is amazing to read of the freedom he allowed everybody
around him. Peter was free. Judas was free. The Prodigal
Son was free. We are free to follow or not follow him, and
we are free when we follow him. Our central freedom is
before God as each of us responds to the Spirit of God. In
marriage each of us has, and must be given, freedom –
freedom to love the other, to obey God and to grow.

   Freedom is also more complex than many of us suppose.

Many choices can be made which start out free, but end in bondage. Millions of marriages are ruined by addiction – alcohol, drugs, sex, food, leisure pursuits, work and consumption are what people freely choose to do, but they enslave. The central issue is clearly stated by Jesus. You cannot serve two masters. If you love and serve God then along with that you have a relationship with the whole of God's creation. These are blessings which are located in the greater scheme of things. But if we focus on something within the creation and choose that *rather than God*, then the lie of idolising a bit of the creation puts us in bondage. It distorts and corrupts the meaning of life, creating *fixated persons*. This applies to marriage, because many of us try to make marriage, or our partner, into the ultimate in life. But the effect is bondage, because marriage cannot carry the ultimate meaning of life. Our partners are mere creatures, miserable sinners like us, and they cannot be a god or goddess for us. Many people today express their freedom especially in their home; it is the focus of much of their lives but it is also their trap. It makes relationships superficial outside and even within the family. It absorbs energy and enslaves – television, meal preparation, adding on room to room. The command to love God with all our heart, strength, mind and soul is the central truth of life and *only* in serving God is perfect freedom.

Third, most of us do not operate with freedom, but with *diminished responsibility*. Responsibility is our ability to respond to God, and this grows as we open our lives before God. Much of the time we are trapped by habit, fatalism, depression, our own personal rigidities and defensiveness from opening up to the challenges posed by daily living and marriage. It takes us twenty years to learn to apologise or look after money properly. Sometimes, we are obsessed, defeated, cannot make decisions and cannot understand what the right choice might be. We need freedom from these weaknesses, not to grow into ego-centred choice, but to become those who really love, and are patient, who care and even suffer to see things through. It is our response to God, our obedience to God's norms which allows us to grow in responsibility. This is not wet freedom, but courageous perseverance which does not allow us to grow weary or lose heart. As each of us lives our life before the Father, responding to the Holy Spirit's guidance, so we experience the growth of responsibility. To each that hath will more be given.

So as persons in marriage we should know freedom from domination and the need to dominate, freedom to serve God and not be bound to things around us and freedom to grow in response ability before God.

Reactive relationships

The weak sense which many people have of their relationship with God is amazing. They are surrounded on every side and even inside themselves with the glory of God's creation. And really the show is stupendous; in human terms the Creator is continually showing off, today with greys and dull greens and dark sculptured trees and tomorrow with brilliant snow and cerulean sky. Each day of scientific research shows the mind-blowing cleverness and brilliance of everything around us. The sense that God has made us and not we ourselves is inescapable. Except God, nothing. And each of us is called to live before God all the days of our life. God's law is our way. Jesus tells us to love our enemies, and pray for those who persecute us. We are not to repay an evil person. Graphically, Jesus tells us that when someone strikes us on the right cheek, we are to turn the other one to him as well (Matt. 5:38–48). We are to do good to those who hate us and not repay evil for evil. Yet many of us live reactive relationships. When evil is done to us, or before it is, we do evil in return. Tit for tat – an eye for an eye – do as you are done by – well, he did it to me – if that's how you want it – after all I've done for you – see if I care. The quality of our relationship does not rise above or fall below that which we experience. Anger, resentment, self-pity, calculation, and even love and happiness are just a reaction to our circumstances and the way we are treated. They are not a response to God, an act of faith, open to God's love, justice, grace and forgiveness. Often these patterns are tired and oppressive. 'If she won't give me sex, why should I care.' 'If he complains again, I'll give him something to complain about.' But the end result is that each of us is overcome by evil. Whatever evil there is in our marriage and circumstances will get to us. Our reactions cannot be better. Jesus's teaching and life travel in the opposite direction; we are to respond to others in God's terms, not theirs. God makes his sun shine on good and evil, and so we must return good for evil. When one (or better, both partners) is not reactive, but feeds God's love and fairness into a marriage, it will get better; the dynamic is towards what is good and joyful. It needs prayer and the obedience which garrots reactive emotions, but it can happen for all of us.

Holiness and wholeness

The wholeness of our existence before God is a truth of creation and our birthright as persons. It is also our response to life: we are to love the Lord our God with all our heart, soul, strength and mind. There is to be nothing of us which is outside our love of God. This is holiness. It is straightforward and it works, and it means that we know a personal wholeness which leaves us at peace with ourselves. Thus runs Augustine's great truth, 'Thou hast made us for thyself alone, and our hearts are restless unless they find their rest in Thee.' Over against this truth, which each of us experience if only by default, there are a whole range of ways in which humanity and culture have sought to divide our personhood. Often some human faculty is given primacy or centrality and another is seen as an opposite or subsidiary tendency. For many people life is seen as a struggle between one or more of these dualisms. A full analysis of them is not possible in this chapter, but the underlying principle is clear. We are called to know our wholeness before God and in holiness of living. If instead we identify ourselves with other than God, we introduce contradictions which are often cultural and principial. They falsely divide us from ourselves and cause us to split, live in tension and know competing principles for living.

In Table 9.1 are set out some of the common dualisms, their cultural backgrounds and the tensions they introduce.

Table 9.1

DUALISM	CULTURE	TENSION
Ideal/Real	Greek. Renaissance Ideals. Models of human perfection. Plato. Hegel	Ideal unattainable. Real aweful. Gender ideals. Live two lives.
Order/Chaos Structure	Greek. Apollo/Dionysius	Rational order imposed by mind on disorder of life.
Purpose/Aimlessness	Greek. Aristotle	Life is goal-orientated or drifting.
Mind/Matter Mind/Body	Greek. Enlightenment. Lucretius	Life is ideas *or* the physical. Thought should control body or body escapes.
Nature/Grace	Middle Ages. Aquinas	Life is natural to be understood in its own terms, except for the bits which belong to God.
Supernatural/Natural	Middle Ages until now	Natural can be understood. Supernatural a matter of blind faith.
Feeling/Thinking Noumena/Phenomena Mind/Soul, Spirit	Enlightenment. Kant	There are some things you understand, but others you have to feel or intuit. Love is blind.

Freedom/Fate Freewill/Determinism	Enlightenment	Life runs you or you run it.
Private/Public Inner Life/Outer Life	Romanticism. Late 19th century subjectivism	Squaring what you feel inside with what's going on outside. Shyness. Nobody understands me. Life seems so unreal. Real me/ public performance.
Theory/Practice Theory/Praxis	19th and 20th C Scientism. Marx	First you think, then you do, or what you do rules what you think.
Freedom/Morality	Victorian era	Morality curbs and wars against freedom, or freedom has to break out of moral straitjacket.
Instincts/Outer Control Id/ Superego	Late 19th C Naturalism McDougall, Freud	There is a continual war between my inner drives and external constraints.
Faith/Understanding	Late 19th and 20th centuries	You understand some things, but religion is a leap of faith.
Being/Acting	18th, 19th, and especially 20th centuries	Activism and the tendency to see life as doing or as contemplative.
Fate/Control	19th and 20th centuries	Either life controls me or I control it. Passivity/need to control.

These dualisms have a deep and destructive effect on the lives of individuals and couples who buy into them. In many marriages the quest for an ideal mate which is entirely unrealistic continues into the marriage and even undermines it. 'If only you were six feet tall, ambitious and a millionaire,' she says, failing to add, 'you would be unbearable.' The wholeness of personhood and relationships is lost in these dualisms.

Personhood and roles

Much of life seems to occur in *roles* like father, husband, employee, neighbour, car driver, provider of pocket money and mender of broken cupboards. Sometimes these are socially prescribed and people are asked to conform to them. Marriage has generated a number of powerful role models to which the participants are often expected to conform. It is interesting to ask where the pressure to conform comes from. Usually, it is self-imposed; the wife or husband feels they have to be like this. Sometimes it comes from the spouse, from family or from broader social pressures. Let us consider these models. There are a number of powerful ones – *the housewife, the male breadwinner, the home manager, the food provider, the emotional support, the children organiser* and *the entertainer* which weigh heavily on people. Many a Jewish mother has been deeply offended when any food that she has provided has been turned down; does Proverbs not say, 'She gets up while it is still dark and provides food for her family and they should be exceedingly grateful'? Many men have carried alone a financial burden for the marriage and family which has caused them ceaseless worry.

Roles are really secondary. Often they are seen with crippling rigidity, and there is something inhuman about living inside a role. Our failure in a role does not destroy us as persons. Whatever we do, we should be able to do fully as people taking up different tasks and responsibilities. When these are shared the division of labour emerges as a process of mutuality and often of great flexibility. The rigidities of roles contrast with the biblical model of mutual help, where people exist first as persons and are never reduced to the status of merely acting out roles. It should be possible for the biblical model of mutual help to prevent anyone from being reduced to the position of merely fulfilling a role in marriage. Throughout, even when there is intense pressure from childcare and work, a deeper personal respect and tenderness should mark the relationship (Borrowdale, 1989).

Domination and accommodation

It is easy for relationships to involve dominance – for one partner to impose their character and will on a relationship. Some people are larger than life and require other people to be smaller than life. The expression of the personality of some people inhibits or imposes on others, and this pattern can happen in marriage on many dimensions. One partner's wants can make demands on the other. Their friendship, worklife, sport or sense of humour can impose on the other. Many marriages experience tussles of the will, where one person's wants or views of things take precedence over the other. Sometimes these kinds of conflict involve small issues – who should clean the bath – at other times they involve choice of jobs, control of money or the way the children are brought up. It is easy in this situation for resolution to occur through domination and accommodation.

Domination occurs through a variety of techniques. One of the most common is anger, irritation. Because the other partner fears anger or even violence, they get their way. Many people who are angry and violent say they cannot help it, but actually use it as a technique for getting their own way. Another is the withdrawal of love. Because love is so powerful, its withdrawal is debilitating. Often it is used as a way of imposing on the other. Its cost, of course, is fear, loss of security and anger at this kind of treatment. The withdrawal of love is always wrong. Domination can also occur through nagging and other forms of manipulation like sulking. These techniques are very common, and the reaction is often to accommodate, to fit in, so that the relationship becomes structured around that imbalance. Later, for a variety of reasons, the loss of personal openness takes its toll.

As Tournier pointed out in his book, *The Strong and the Weak* (1963), the strong in this pattern are not. They are displaying patterns of weakness which impose on their partner. The biblical pattern is one of mutual submission, where each partner pools will, wishes, ambitions and goals. The central direction is a concern that God's will be done and that the partner is counted more important than themselves. This is really worth working for.

Living in the Spirit

It is incredible how much human beings rigidify. They settle down into their way, their habits and their understanding. Partners become, or seem, boring. There is a loss of the personal quality of life, of its depth and significance; yet this should not be so. All of us should be alive to God, continually living out the dynamic of faith, facing new choices and possibilities every day. Being open to God is always the greatest challenge in life, because God is so much greater than we are. As persons who live in an open relationship with God, we should continually know the dynamics of life with God in our marriages and persons. There should be freedom before God, holiness of living which is liberating, a wholeness of life and a freedom from and towards domination. We should never be rigid. There should be no problem which is beyond addressing. The possibilities of change are endless, if our lives are open to God. The 'if' is so big.

10

GENDER AND MARRIAGE

The changing discussion

Marriage is the institution where much of the most profound contact between women and men takes place. In each generation they are brought together in intimate relationships which deeply shape much of what it means to be human. In many cultures there is a high degree of gender segregation and polarisation which can make this process quite formal, but in all cultures it is deeply significant. In order to get our bearings on this fundamental theme we need to recall some of the debate and themes which have opened up in this area.

First, we recall the central biblical perspective. It is of the created unity and complementarity of humankind as woman and man before God. They are mutual 'helpmeets', share humanity, and are created either man or woman. Sexual identity is not just biological, but is part of the created character of each of us. As such it is good, rich with human potential, within and outside marriage and is affirmed as part of the deliberate will of God for human life. However, human sin throughout biblical and world history has been especially marked by hostility and alienation between the sexes. Biblical narrative, until the life of Jesus, shows this evil and its consequences. The main form has been male domination through the abuse of physical and economic power, disrespect and lustful sex. Women, like Delilah with Sampson, have the same capacity for evil and treachery, but historically less opportunity. In the life and relationships of Jesus we see the tough healing of this great fracture in gender relationships. He brought men and women together and broke down the dividing wall of hostility.

Each generation thinks it invents gender, but it has been around for a long time. The old orthodoxy on gender was that in the past women were oppressed and things have progressively got better. In one way this is true. Reductions in family size through contraception have taken pressure off women. Washing machines have improved things for men and women but relationships are always more than technology, and as we have reflected on the social position of women and men two responses have indicated that this process is not automatic. One development has been a growing historical awareness of the fact that there was much good in earlier attitudes. Protestantism especially has raised and transformed the status of women and wives. There was an explanation of these attitudes. They grew out of the central biblical precept of mutuality, and it was reflected in the social position of women. Women were heirs of the Christian faith, were given freedom to choose to marry, were protected from predatory sex, were honoured in weddings, marriage and motherhood, were acknowledged as having callings as missionaries, nurses and teachers and were seen as worthy of Christian education. Although the picture is complex, with Christian repression also occurring, it is clear that there has been a strong Christian reform movement which helps explain much that is good about the position of women in the West (Hersh, 1978; Gaebelein Hull, 1987).

The other development has been feminist reflection. Early feminists pointed out that the progressive model was far too optimistic and inaccurate. Men did little housework, often ditched their wives, had a record of rape and strongly protected their own status. Their scholarship revealed that, in biblical terms, the sinful male agenda of exploitation and pride was far more deeply rooted and complex than had been allowed. The depth of the problem was far greater than could be solved by a little progress. Gender differences of language, psychology, relationship style, values, understanding, faith and thought were shown to be deep, and caused not by biology, but by assumptions made in a male culture which could be questioned and even overthrown. For example, males had thought of history largely in terms of political power and conflict, but women in terms of relationships and personal life stories. Christian feminists noted that much of the New Testament takes the latter form, moving under the history of the Roman Empire and the Jewish nation into a concern with people's faith, life and relationships. It was clear that these differences needed to be unpacked.

But what did they mean to feminists? Were they cultural differences which would melt into sameness? Was there an inalienable gulf between men and women? Was there only hope with women? Increasingly there were a complex set of feminist reactions which had no coherent direction. The idea of a Women's Movement disappeared and both men and women were left struggling with the question of what it is to be a man or a woman biologically and culturally. The answers took a number of forms. Male and female were seen as different and opposite principles – drawing on Eastern deities. Women were seen as competing, individually or collectively with men in a power struggle which had an open-ended outcome. Male and female were seen as biologically natural roles – the woman as nurturer and the man as predator. Or gender was seen as a cultural construction which needed deconstructing. There were problems with each of these positions, as they missed the biblical truths of the created complementarity and difference of men and women and the alienation caused by sin. It is perhaps fair to say that there is a lostness now in these positions.

Male gender myths

This chapter will take a particular line through this debate. The next two sections will look at gender idioms which husbands and wives have tended to adopt in Western culture which create marital tensions. These tensions can and need to be understood, shared and dissipated by a deeper union, sharing and trust. Let us therefore identify some of these.

Men and work

Traditionally men have divided life into work and home. This rhythm is deep in our souls. There are two corollaries of this. First, when work is involved, anything else is a distraction – wife, children, communication and concern often cease. There is the strong myth that men should only think of one thing at a time. Concentration, the segregation of time units, withdrawal for work are seen as compelling needs. And really, here lies the rub, only men work. Now concentration and work matter, and men do much of both, but the fallacies of this approach are many. The rest of life cannot always stop while work takes place. Wives are often asked to do the multifaceted work, so that husbands are not distracted, and wives work as well. Second, the male myth is work *and* leisure. He comes home to rest; it is his right, and she comes home to more work. Male fixations in work have spoiled many marriages and the principle of shared work and co-operation is often not experienced.

Men and play

From an early age men are taught to play – marbles, Monopoly, football, basketball. Boys 'go out to play' for much of their early years, and become experts at games and their rules. Many men now earn their living through play, often watched by other men. Moreover, games are addictive for three reasons: you get better at them and they become a celebration of your skill; the outcome is uncertain and the outcome is not threatening. They seem to offer a retreat from the threats, stress and problems of life and many men build this retreat into their lives and marriages. It is a zone of securty and comfort which can be impenetrable and inexplicable to wives. The golf widow is quite a universal experience in the male game-playing culture. The security and peace should be, and can be, in the marriage, not in playing games.

But there is another level of this phenomenon. Men can learn to treat life as a game, to distance it. 'We don't have to be too serious about this, do we?' There is disengagement and life is a bit of a laugh. Often this is a way of treating failure or insoluble problems. Make it a bit of a joke. There are wives who find themselves unable to get inside this myth. Issues that should be talked through or addressed are addressed in silly ways. Bitterly, life is a game; it doesn't matter.

Man as hero

Life, films, novels, sport and media continually offer men as heroes – Odysseus, Wellington, Pele, Clint Eastwood and thousands of others have offered models for the role down the centuries. Being a hero is reassuring. Women, or just your wife, find you attractive. Weakness disappears. You can believe in yourself. Boys are taught to hero-worship and aspire to grow into this pattern, or experience it vicariously. It is, of course, a lie, built on the Greek man–god heroes, and its cost is deep. Many men believe in themselves to the extent that they cannot acknowledge and face failings which are quite easy to see. They are not mega-heroes, but have little claims on which their identity hangs and which need to be defended. Wives either support the illusion or threaten the identity. Of course, none of us needs more than the faithfulness of God and the love of those who are honest with us, but the heroic lie, and the failures which follow from it, are often costly in husband–wife relationships.

Man as strong

Men are often taught to be strong. This means physical strength, psychological control, courage and the exercise of power. Men often feel that if they are in control, then everything will be fine. If you can keep your nerve when all around are losing theirs, you'll be a man, my son. The solution is therefore often to impose male will on the situation. 'My will be done' is the unwritten rule of relationships and transactions. The costs of this are enormous. Rape, sexual aggression, anger and violence often occur because men believe that their control and power are the answer. They can see no other solution. Disastrous patterns often follow from this macho view; male solutions which are wrong cannot be challenged without undermining the order of the universe. By contrast, the strength that counts is the strength to love, care, forgive and repent. These gentle powers of the Holy Spirit are as far removed from many male conceptions of strength as Jesus Christ is from a machine gun.

Husband as breadwinner

Male financial provision for the family has often been a strong myth, yet today employment is often insecure. Often this is a lonely and anxious burden. It may involve staying in a soul-destroying job. For some it is more acute because it involves being successful, providing an affluent lifestyle for wife and family, and guaranteeing certain kinds of consumption. For some men it involves pretence about money and the failure to acknowledge and face debt. The fears which surround this role, sometimes engendered by the wife's demands, are considerable. We have all heard stories of men who have pretended to go to work long after losing their job, because they could not face sharing what had happened. When a couple face unemployment and poverty together, most of the problems can be solved or put in place. The real problem is often the isolated view of the male breadwinner and the idiom of the male as economic success. If he is a success, the problems are even greater, because the underlying idea can become that this, not love and faithfulness, is the basis of the marriage.

Husband as rational

Men have often been trained to *think* and believe themselves to be experts in ideology, logic, theory, mathematics, business, computing and public affairs. They often master technical, professional and academic languages, and become experts in one area of thought. Few well-known philosophers have been women. This process is, of course, cultural, and its biases are evident. What is 'rational' in one era has frequently been shown to be nonsense in the next; thinkers often get it wrong. Men often think about things, but tend to ignore relationships. An expert in chess or computing can think like a tortoise in other areas. Abstract patterns of thought cannot cope with immediate problems. And much thought is often ego-centred or self-justificatory. Thus, many male patterns of thought are problematic in ways which impinge on a marriage. Many men will think about tidying up, but not do it. They cannot relate. Their language is complex. They are at a loss outside specialisms. They need to be right, to win arguments. In many marriages male intellectual arrogance struggles against the biblical truth that humility before God is the pre-condition for all wisdom. Husbands often find it hard to change their minds, especially when their wives are right.

Man as creative

The arts have often been effectively owned by the male of the species. Human creativity, often whipped up into a mystique, is largely owned by men as artists, musicians, singers, actors or even as gardeners, model-makers, cooks and hairdressers. Women cook meals, but men are chefs. Men design kitchens and women use them. Often this idea of creativity is something of a quest. 'I did it my way' is a kind of route to immortality, whether through symphony or topiary. The gender norm in this idiom is for the male to be creative and the woman to be passive – he is the artist; she, the model; he does the painting, she clears up afterwards. Often the male will expect to do what is permanent – DIY or landscape gardening, while the wife does repetitive work which seems to disappear, because it is 'just' service. But, again, the idea and the quest are misplaced. Real creativity belongs only to God and husbands and wives are called to get on with their given lives, which should include for both the interesting and the routine.

Men and outdoors

Gender and territory are fascinating. Men own the outdoors – land, public and natural spaces. This is not just a continuatin of cavewoman and the hunting man, but the long-term identification of women with hearth, home, nurture and housework, and men with farm, factory, road and railway. This has many expressions. Often the male is seen as defending home and wife against other predatory men. Of course, recent more careful history has shown that this pattern is often contradicted. African women work in the fields, many women work in factories and some women ride horses. But many gender relations are marked by *domain*, and his is outdoors. Shooting in North America, Scotland and France is his activity, and so is fishing, golf, mountaineering, potholing, birdwatching (most twitchers are men) and sailing. Car or motorbike signals control of the great outdoors. The male tends the barbecue, while the woman cooks indoors. Or the woman controls the house, while the man goes down the shed or the pub. She is Arthur Daly's 'Her Indoors'. Many of these domains are marked by hostility and can be oppressive for the partner. They are kept in or pushed out, because there is no intent to share lives and space.

Action man

The male obsession with action is amazing. American films are full of inarticulate males going from one frenzy of activity to another. Sport, driving, achieving, record-break-ing, running, stimulants and fitness cults all cry action. Of course, many males are passive action men, watching others at sport or work, but the idiom remains overwhelming. They have been taught to do, rather than relate. Sharing, explor-ing a relationship, establishing understanding, meeting and keeping in contact are often lower on the male agenda than the female one. They do and freak out. Meanwhile the wife waits for communication and sharing, for doing in order to relate, rather than relating in order to do.

There are other powerful myths which capture male marital culture, but all of them have a similar pattern. They move the husband away from his full personhood before God into being a worker, a success, in control, a hero or a joker, but in so doing they close off the full sharing of marriage. The cause may be fear or defeat. They also succeed in parodying the wife and her love. The conse-quence is a woman who knows she has not shared her man.

Women's idioms in marriage

Woman as sex object

Women are taught, for this is part of our culture, that they are wives because they are sexually attractive. The cosmet-ics, fashion, sex and hairdressing industries convey this and it is built into the self-conception of many wives. It is demeaning to them as persons and to their husbands. We vastly underestimate the extent to which modern promis-cuous relationships have surrounded sex with fear. Wives who need to stay looking young, who fear other women and who do not trust their husband cannot easily enjoy sharing their bodies with him. Being the person who is there for sex is not being a person. Yet many women psychologically inhabit such a space. Quite probably their husband's love of them extends to hair-rollers, vomiting and a Zimmer-frame, but the myth of sex object controls and limits them as persons and removes the joy from sex as a genuine expression of love.

Woman as homemaker

Many wives see themselves as the one who looks after husband and children and this is their *raison d'être*. The Jewish wife feeds her husband into obesity. Housework is a sacred ritual which gives meaning to life and expands to fit the time available. In many traditional families this attitude is seen as almost a sacred obligation, and many men require care of them to be the ultimate priority. How sad is the lack of sense of self-worth and freedom in this attitude. Jesus's words to Martha about this attitude to housework ring down the centuries. 'Mary', spending time with Jesus, 'has chosen what is better, and it will not be taken away from her' (Luke 10:42). There are appalling husbands who have required this dutiful role and have then gone off with a woman whom they have found 'more interesting'.

Many wives approach this role more aggressively. They become strong consumers, pushing for continuously higher levels of consumption in the home, which represent their own status to friends, neighbours and family. They also control much of this domain, dishing out food for compliance and using the home as a way of organising the family. Extended family, friendship networks and domestic requirements then control family members and create matriarchal family dominance. He takes off his shoes when he comes in, for he stands on her ground.

Relationship controller

Many women have also seen themselves as the one who sorts out relationships. Dad may be irritable, but Mother will point out to the children that he is just tired. Sometimes the men will be inarticulate about relationships and know little of what is going on, but the wife will network and sort things out. She will often know what he is like, will interpret what is going on in his relationships and even try to programme them. 'Just sign this card.' There are many families where the Mother is, and perhaps needs to be, the hub around which people revolve. It is a position of power and can easily create problems for the husband, son-in-law and others. Like the Wife of Bath the woman really understands relationships and relies on this as a source of power and dominance. In these situations it is easy for the woman not to understand what is going on, or to presume. The result is a series of stereotypes for the man which prevent the depth of a relationship really opening up.

Flatterer support

Here the myth fits the tendency of men to be dominant, and presumably stupid. The status quo is maintained by flattering the male ego. Life is kept ordered by cosseting the male and convincing him that everything is fine. Many jobs have this structure. Often the Secretary/Personal Assistant has this role. The agreement is that *his* work is important and hers is to support *him*. This flattery means that personal problems which the man has are unaddressed. Often they are pushed down the list of what is important to him. 'When I'm less busy, I'll attend to this.' The self-importance means that respect for others, and especially for the wife, is likely to deteriorate. Her work and significance are likely to be ignored by this rampant male ego.

The emotional subjective woman

This myth has long been projected by men who see themselves as cool, detached, not easily swayed. But its cultural weight is so great that it still shapes many relationships. He sees the bigger picture; she does not. He claims to be unemotional, when he is emotional like her. She is invited to retreat into the small world of home and childcare, where she will not develop the tools of understanding and wider awareness which could make her contribution different. Because she is not in control, she expresses emotion, but cannot make decisions. He makes decisions, but abhors emotion. He learns to push her until she breaks down and needs comforting in a way that reasserts his control. How deep the damage this idiom does to women and men.

The gender polarisation

The result of these myths, despite the massive changes generated by feminism, and partly because of them, is a continued polarisation of gender attitudes reflected in marriage. In Table 10.1 are some of the attitudes which many couples appropriate.

Table 10.1

Aspects of male culture	*Aspects of women's culture*
Action as goal-orientated, achievement	Action as task to be done
Talk as conveying ideas, expression of thought	Talk as relating, sharing experience
Competitive	Co-operative
Likes to be able to concentrate on a single task	Is used to doing a number of things at the same time
Differentiates sharply between work and leisure	Finds work and leisure often interrelate
Rests and opts out in well-defined ways	Snatches rest and leisure times
Strong, silent man	Talkative, expressive female
Dominant, talkative man	Supportive, listening woman

Concerned about truth, correctness of ideas	Concerned about ideas in context, what is going on
Interested in the appearance of women, not men	Concerned about their own dress, appearance
Ethics of right actions	Ethics of right relationships
Emotions are largely inexpressible	Emotions can be discussed, and need to be
Ideal of strong, large size, mature	Ideal of young, thin and soft
Operates through organisational structures	Operates through networking
Lives in instrumental relationships	Believes in relationships *per se*
Posts them	Writes Christmas and birthday cards
Has high-tech camera, video	Takes holiday snaps etc. with simple camera
Does larger creative jobs at home	Is responsible for repetitive tasks at home
Takes on unthinking domestic manual tasks	Maintains control of domestic organisation
Is responsible for children through the mother	Is directly responsible for the children
Aesthetic sense functional and austere	Aesthetic sense colour and harmony
Learns through books	Learns through discussion
Language is self-expressive	Language is coded, relational
Cooks like chef	Cooks meals
Concerned about employment	Concerned with inflation
Christian focus on words and doctrine	Christian focus on worship and community

These myths are formative and take a great deal of awareness to unpack. Often they are part of the richness and play of a relationship, but it needs trust across gender barriers and a level of mutual awareness and sharing which does not settle down into male or female myths. Sometimes this does not happen.

11

THE EMOTIONS OF MARRIAGE

A Christian understanding of emotions

Our emotional life is complex, varied and quite often unstable. It is worth spending a little time in locating the place of emotions in our life. First, we must demolish the split some people try to make between feelings and thinking. Feelings involve thought; fear arises because we work out consequences or through reflection on the past. Liking someone probably arises from our own values, preferences and ways of thinking. In this sense emotions are often direct summaries of patterns of thought in our lives – the place where thoughts get knotted. But they are more: they are also personal, can be good, can often be trusted and reflect our commitments and responses. They are a created part of our personhood in which much of the commentary on life takes place. We feel tired, because our body *is*. We are joyful, because this friendship or day is *good*. We feel depressed, because there seems no way of sorting out this problem. This wholesome *created* role for emotions is good and reflects the nature of life as a playing orchestra reflects a musical score.

But even this interpretation is a bit flat, because emotions are intensely personal. They reflect *my* life. Especially they reflect, although many people do not acknowledge this, people's central relationship with God. Peace, striving, love, anger, joy, fear and indifference are tied in with our response to God and processes of development which occur throughout life. A theology of emotions uncovers the fact that God calls people to develop emotionally in some ways and not in others. Anger is not to be harboured, but care and patience are. So our lives can develop an emotional tone which may, or may not be, godly and holy.

That is not to say that we control our emotions. In fact, people divide quite sharply on this issue. Some do try to control their emotional lives – by thinking, by the planning of life or by emotional suppression. Often this is cultural: an Italian, or a Geordie, perhaps has a more expressive emotional content to what they say than a Londoner. Even this is complicated, for emotions can be loud or quiet, expressed or private. But emotional suppression never quite works. Something is always going on which sooner or later surfaces. Suppression *is* an emotional state. It is being 'cool', or 'having a stiff upper lip' or 'being white with rage'. Other people see themselves as being controlled by their emotions. They opt for the roller-coaster. But this doesn't fully work either, because people find ways of manipulating their emotions – 'having a high' or finding 'excitement' or 'falling in love'. Emotions grow from life rather than defining it. Thus these two humanist options of being controlled by or controlling our feelings do not adequately address the relationship of life and emotions.

The biblical perspective is bigger. It recognises the place of our emotions in relation to God, the full content of our lives, our ways of thought and our relationships. They can be brought to God, for the deepest truth of our emotions is to be found, as the Psalmist recognised, in the relationship which God has with us. The Bible also gives us the tools for understanding the distortion of emotions which occurs through sin. There are a range of ways through which sinful emotional patterns are habituated in us and grip us, and freeing ourselves from these is one of the big challenges of man's relationships. It is easy to be stuck in an emotional response which is no longer truthful. For example, some emotional failures occur because issues which belong to God are retained by human beings; what remain God's judgement we take over as our vengeance;

walking faithfully before God becomes our anxiety to control life. Other problems occur because our emotions are *self*-focused and a law unto themselves rather than being submitted to God – self-importance rules, we need to be happy, or we are locked in self-pity. Other emotions are simply wrong, or even evil, like self-congratulation, complacency, hate, the need to conform, irritation. The attitudes which generate them are faulty and they merely spawn another range of problems. One of the tasks in this study will be therefore to look at the healthy created patterns of marital life and at the pathological patterns which are destructive. On the one hand, we may be experiencing emotional lives which are themselves generating marital problems, and on the other, there may be good news about how they can be addressed.

The past

In many, perhaps most, marriages partners experience situations where the emotional note of their relationship is not in tune with the actual situation. Sometimes, of course, the wrong note may be expected; he comes home early and virtuous, but she has been tidying his mess all day. But there are other times where however he expresses his love she is still angry, or whatever she does, she is still to blame. It may seem as though something is going on in the relationship, but really it is coming from outside, and especially from the past. It may be the past in the relationship, where it signifies a sense of the intractability of the problem and the sense of defeat, or it may be from further back.

Here, especially, we must reflect on what it is like to be a child. Fresh, young, close to the ground, flexible, crying loudly at hurt or hunger, enjoying most things and learning to sum up a situation in our own terms, but understanding very little. The emotional tenor of relationships is easily read by a child. Mummy is irritable. Dad is soft just now.

They are trying to fob me off with toys. But there are many things to be learned about life and relationships. Excitement easily spills into tears. If making a fuss works, I'll try some more. Through trial, error, adjustment and with a little guidance children grow into emotional adulthood. Except where there is trauma. For some things happen to children or give them experiences with which they cannot cope. A child who has loved her father, finds that he has gone. He has left Mummy and has left me. Mummy is not getting him back. I will wait for him to say 'Goodnight' to me. What did I do to make him leave me? I feel alone. Mummy is so sad. The child cannot possibly have the resources to deal with this desertion. Or a parent is angry or abusive, repeatedly and perhaps violently. The child asks, 'What have I done wrong?' but the question cannot be answered, because the anger has been carried from somewhere else and is being vented on the child. There is no answer to the child's question. The only understanding is that the problem lies elsewhere than with the child. Yet the child must bear the burden. He is forced to blame himself, when the problem lies elsewhere. The seriouness of these experiences is beyong telling. Jesus said, 'You would better have a millstone tied round your neck and be thrown into the sea than to do this to a child.'

The result is that the child carries a problem which reflects their right understanding of what life should be like, but without understanding and which is too big for them. It is often fundamentally debilitating and often the unguided emotional responses are awry. The abused child blames herself. How wrong. The deserted child fears he has upset his father, when the truth is the other way round. The deserted child expresses anger to the deserted mother. So the emotional traps are sprung and these problems generate secondaries, like cancer. The parent who is desperate for peace faces a clinging unpeaceful child. The person who could be loved feels worthless and unconsolably lonely. The abused person feels too cowed ever to stand up for her own respect and is spotted by another abuser. Or the abused person vents their anger on an innocent person who does not really understand. These kinds of problems, and there are many of them, some far less obviously someone's fault, often play havoc in later marriage relationships. Often they result in *transference*, the process whereby emotions are inappropriately directed at someone else, often the spouse. The scale of these problems resulting from family breakdown is vast; it has created personal damage on a scale that far exceeds that of World War Two.

Addressing them is crucial and this often involves counselling and understanding, the exposing of weaknesses and failures which the child could not understand and face. But it also involves bringing these issues to God. This is not just a matter of internal psychological manipulation, for the issues are real, and wrong has consequences. These issues must be taken to the only place where they have been truly faced, the Cross of Christ. The Psalms show the process. The evil must be addressed by pouring out our hearts before God. (Ps. 62:8). This involves acknowledging the hurt, anger and defeat, and recognising, if it is true, that we have been wronged, and if we were a child, that it was not my fault. The issue is then God's, no longer ours, and we then wait. God may restore our soul. We may be given a renewed sense of wholeness and holiness before God. There is nothing wrong with us, as we were led to believe. We may be given the power to forgive and even restore relationships. We may know the blessing that comes to those who suffer evil and persecution but allow it to go no further. And we will know something of the content of Jesus's words on the Cross, as naked with nails through his arms and legs, he said, 'Father forgive them, they know not what they do' (Luke 23:34).

The transmission of sin from one generation to the next is always the biggest problem of the human race. Ezekiel quotes the proverb, 'The fathers have eaten sour grapes, and the children's teeth are set on edge' (Ezek. 18:2) and shows how God reupdiates it. We can be renewed. We can turn from failure and defeat before God. We each, *in relation to God*, can live our own life and marriages. We cannot be slaves to the past and get ourselves a new heart and a new spirit.

Bonding and feeling together

Some people feel shy. The act of meeting another person or group is one of great self-consciousness and perhaps confusion. For others the process of meeting is so routine, that it seems not to engage their feelings at all. Yet meeting, let alone living together, does generate a great deal of emotional activity and reaction. Marriage marks the beginning of a different kind of emotional life where in principle a whole range of emotions are shared, and another range are interactive. This is a very profound process, and it can also be difficult.

Many emotions are generated by *arguing* and *conflict*. Often, it is difficult for us to understand why we are arguing as we are. There are many reasons for it.

1. I am tired.
2. I dislike the other person.
3. I am being ignored.
4. He needs to be put down.
5. She is not listening.
6. I am upset.
7. He irritates me and will not change.
8. She doesn't care.
9. A different point is more important.
10. He doesn't live like that.
11. I don't want an argument,
12. I can't discuss what's really on my mind.
13. I want to avoid this topic.
14. I want to get my own way.

Most of them arise because there is a breakdown of sharing and trust, and the bigger point is not the argument, but what has generated the aggression. Many arguments become ritualised and create fear. Often couples retreat from any kind of robust discussion or disagreement to avoid quarrels. The question is why the quarrels really arise. Disagreement should be no personal threat, if it has not been invested with emotional blame and anger.

Many of these difficulties are easy to understand, although more difficult to address. If someone is used to hiding his or her feelings, then they cannot easily be shared. It is possible to *act*, to *distance*, to *construct boundaries*, to *emotionally withdraw* and to use *barriers*. Actually, we use techniques like this much of the time, and the question is why. Is it selfishness, tiredness, fear or lack of love? If a person feels only their own feelings and has no empathy with others, then sharing is going to be difficult; sometimes we are egocentric in the construction of our feelings. If the expression of emotions of a certain kind or in a certain way is taboo, then they will usually not be expressed. Often, too, the interpretation of feelings runs on tramlines; he thinks she is always getting at me, while she is trying to find out what is wrong. These are particular problems which can be worked through with a little love and awareness. But there is a range of other problems which reflects the culture of our age more fully.

For many of us in an individualistic culture sharing our lives seems an impossible task. Many have had the bonding with one or more parent broken; they have partly been left alone. Two parents in paid work and frequent exposure to media have made children used to daydreaming and subjective isolation rather than forming relationships. In many homes individuals operate out of separate rooms. And the forms of thought we are invited to adopt are egocentric – my needs and wants. But with time, love and talking, no more, real togetherness and emotional sharing are always possible.

Love

Love is more than emotion. It is the truth of our existence before God. But the emotion of love is very simple and wholehearted. It is being *for* this person. In Paul's words, just as we wash, feed, rest and dress our own bodies, so we desire to nourish and cherish this other person. Always, we are either for or against this person, and we should always be for.

But in our culture the emotional content of love is frequently very confused. For example, someone may say, 'I wanted a better husband, but now I have got him, I suppose I've got to put up with him.' Apart from being an insult to God and dishonouring the other person, this attitude makes the expression of love always some kind of failure. It is half-hearted. Or a man may try to manipulate the love of a wife. If she shows love she is rewarded by fun and attention and if she does not, she is punished by silence and sulking. Then his emotions are not *his*, but are to evoke responses from her. Many of us are surprised by how close love and anger seem to be but actually this is not the case. Wanting to be loved and anger are close, for often when we feel that we are not loved, we react in anger. But wanting to be loved is not love. Often we mistake for love the desire to be happy, feelings of elation, an ideal relationship, escape from loneliness, a sense of self-respect and self-awareness, giving and receiving attention, but love is just love, love for this other person, love which is patient, which does not insist on its own way and desires, which has joy in what is good for this other person. It is possible for the emotional garbage of love to drop away and the steadfast love in which couples flower and grow together to emerge as an overwhelming truth of life.

Emotional hiss

Most of us generate a great deal of emotional hiss. We have attitudes of selfishness, self-pity, wilfulness and irritation which give off emotional messages which are often very off-putting. The tone of these messages is clear. Partners can read them clearly. 'I need some peace and quiet; please go away from me.' 'Why can't you pull your weight around the house?' 'I've had another boring day while you have been enjoying yourself.' When we consider the nature of these messages, there is clearly something which needs communicating. There may well be substance in all of these messages but because they stay as emotional hiss, a feeling which is conveyed to the partner, but unaddressed, they merely create emotional distance and blame and they can easily be misinterpreted. The plea, 'I need some peace and quiet' can easily be read as 'Why don't you pull your weight?', especially by a guilty husband. In this situation it is easy for couples just to respond to one another's emotional hiss, rather than to one another.

Often the underlying attitudes need addressing. The biblical emphasis on being poor in spirit, meek, pure in heart and a peacemaker, and the even more radical insistence on dying to self underline the problem of the self and its egocentricity. Hart's *Me, Myself and I* (1992) tackles this issue but often we cannot hear our own messages. We radiate irritation, but we feel reasonable. Our voice sounds continually full of self-pity, and is, but we think we are just having an ordinary conversation. Or we ask what the time is, and it is heard as the hiss of blame. This underlines how right are the biblical virtues of honesty, meekness and purity. Pure relationships work; they don't generate misunderstanding and fog. Sadly, we often cannot see that good living is deeper than our own understanding, and obedience to God is the sure route to peaceful and harmonious relationships. It's time piety was rediscovered.

Fear and intimacy

Fear is the most subtle of emotions. Most of us are quite
keen on inducing fear, because it is part of the business of
getting our own way. If the other person is fearful, then we
will tend to have power over them. Parents often discipline
by threats and fear inducing punishment, and children often
see through the technique; last week I saw a mother giving
her child empty and unrealistic threats which the child
happily ignored. But many of our relationship techniques
have this pattern. Getting angry is usually a technique, a
way of inducing fear, and getting one's own way. As opposed
to the Lord's Prayer which submits centrally to the will of
God, there is the assertion of my will over the other person
through inducing fear. Although people who become angry
and even violent feel and assert that it is an unfortunate loss
of self-control, it is often a loss *because it works*. The
underlying motive is the need to have and exercise power.
Anger, aggression, nagging, crying, being upset and silence
can be used to induce fear and submission. The greatest
weapon is the withdrawal of love. Because love is so
powerful, its withdrawal is debilitating. Many generals,
prime ministers and industrial barons live in acute fear of
their wife's withdrawal of love.

But people do not just live in fear, they institutionalise
and cope with it. Defences build up. Desensitising, defences,
non-disclosure and protection occur. Areas of life where a
person may be vulnerable are concreted over. Most sexual
problems crucially involve fear and its suppression. And
fear displaces love, because it undermines the ability to give.
It requires that the other person be treated as the enemy. It
means that a relationship always takes place through a
barrier. Will he criticise me, make me look small, frown or
shout? A couple may copulate naked in bed, but be living
with layers of defensive material between them. Fear
destroys intimacy and openness; it means that although a

couple is together, they do not feel together. Many marital emotions involve constructions which are generated by fear and emphasise, and even exaggerate separation. But there is no fear in love and perfect love casts out fear (1 John 4:18). Patterns of fear, from within the marriage or outside, can be deconstructed. There is to be no exercise of power, no techniques to intimidate; each partner is for the other, and only the fear of God and obedience to God's law of love rule. And we know that the fear of God is without fear, because we are invited to come to God as Abba, as Daddy. When a couple can know and be known without fear, then gentle intimacy replaces distance, and a couple is truly together.

It would probably not be an understatement to say that many people are living with a free-wheeling emotional life which is in some considerable state of crisis. The hiss of emotions, knee-jerks from the past or fear dog daily living. The answer to these emotional problems lies deeper than our emotions. Our emotions must dwell in the truth. In marriage this means in the truth of trust, love and faithfulness and in openness to God.

12

MARRIAGE AND WORK

The structure of the issue

For many people marriage and paid work are the most important elements in their daily lives, and the relationship between the two is bound to be significant. A central starting-point is the fact that, because marriage is a union, whatever one partner does in paid and unpaid work affects the other. If she has had a bad day at the office, it matters to him. In order to see this matter clearly, we need a number of models and definitions. The *male breadwinner* model is a good place to start. Here the husband works in full-time paid employment and the wife is fully involved in housework and childcare. There is a distinct division of labour. Many Western marriages have moved over to a *two-job marriage*. Here husband and wife both work in paid employment and, in degrees, share home tasks. For some people jobs are careers; they involve heavy, long-term commitments. We shall, therefore, also be looking at *one* and *two career marriages*, and at *commuter marriages*. Paid work, the focus of this chapter, is but part of fuller meaning of work in our lives. We shall consider *paid work, housework, family work, rest* and *leisure* as significant areas to consider.

The argument of the chapter is that there are four major trends in the relation between work and marriage.

1. Many couples are moving from the traditional pattern of male breadwinner to a more companionate form of work and marriage. In many ways this move is healthy,

but it involves tensions, the traditional pattern still works for many, and the new form has problems.

2. Two-career marriages have a tendency to overwork and overuse resources. The pressures from employers are often intense, especially for the young, and are undermining marriages.

3. Some are un- or underemployed as couples and have limited resources for their marriage.

4. The present ethos of paid work is creating a work-as-pressure versus marriage as consumption/leisure idiom, which is undermining the character of marriage and family relationships.

To address these problems we need to change our attitudes to work and the home in ways which are crucial for Western civilisation, for the present view of *the consumer home* is destroying the planet, marriages and families. This may seem an overstatement, and many particular families do not have specific problems, but it is a deadly problem.

The male breadwinner

Through much of the world this is the way in which marriages work. The man works long hours in order to provide for his wife and family. He gives her all his effort and she supports him by hers. This faithful reciprocity has been built into millions of good marriages. In India there is a tremendous pattern of care and commitment which men have had to provide for their wives. Hard, poorly paid work is the gift which the husband gives his wife, and it is cherished and honoured as a sign of love. The same occurs in many other cultures. In the coal mining towns of Yorkshire the mutuality is described thus by Dennis, Henriques and Slaughter. The home provides

a haven for the tired man when he returns from work; here he expects to find a meal prepared, a room clean and tidy, a seat comfortable and warm, and a wife ready to give him just what he wants – in fact, the very opposite of the place he has just left, with its noise, dirt, darkness, toil, impersonalism and no little discomfort.

(Dennis *et al.*, 1959, 178).

This pattern can be an expression of love and sharing, especially if the world of his work and her home are both part of community experience. But it also has its potential sources of weakness. One is that it creates *gender-segregated lifestyles*. He mixes with males and she with females and the two groups do not understand one another. There may also be *zones of privacy*. Third, it can create *passive fathers* who withdraw from direct involvement in home and childcare. Separation can occur. He has business trips, conferences, times at the pub and relationships which are outside the marriage, and she talks about her husband to her friends in ways which are different from when he is about. Crucial are the motives and attitudes of each partner. The marriage and one another should be honoured in all they do, and the contributions should be shared.

In the West there has been a class reversal. The old blue-collar working-class pattern was the male breadwinner with wife as homemaker. Now such couples are often both working, full or part-time, to extend the joint income. By contrast, it is business, executive and managerial families where the segregation of roles is most developed. He can command a high income and can afford to fund the home and family on his salary and she stays at home. This *career male executive* is important. Often such couples have nice homes which are out in the suburbs, and they are thus commuter marriages. These have their own character. Usually they involve substantial travel times of, say, two hours daily for the husband. He works in the City or at the office, and there is a split between home and work. At work he has or seeks high status. He may have support staff as secretaries and other employees. There is pressure for self-advancement and self-importance. Certain skills are highly valued. Competition is often built into work and relationships. Hierarchies exercise power. Conspicuous rewards are given – cars, meals, outings and pay. Travel, moving for promotion and long hours are often seen as a prior claim on a person's life. This culture is a poor training for a good sensitive marital relationship. It tends to produce men who are self-important, expect to be looked after, overwork and give automatic priority to their paid work. Home and leisure are often seen as a reward for work, and the wife is expected to fit in with this model. Often strained emotions generated by this ethos are damped at home or need long recovery periods. The wife may also be expected to be a social support to the job and can find that her work, paid or unpaid, is assumed to have a lower status than her husband's. This is the pressure from the culture, although many husbands and executive wives are far better than the model. It is not unknown for the male, affirmed at work, but not by his ignored wife, to pathetically fall into the arms of his secretary or colleague. When couples identify this general problem it is important that they see where the root of the problem is, namely with the *self-important male culture* of many businesses and offices.

When couples operate with this division of labour more generally there is a need for the husband to share and understand what the wife is doing and to recognise that *she and his work have equal importance before God and for each other*. There should also be a sharing of his work by visits, chats, meeting colleagues so that this area of life is not private.

The two-job marriage

Increasingly husbands and wives both have paid work. Wives predominantly take time off while children are young, but this time is relatively short in the small family in the

West, and round that window a higher proportion of wives and mothers work for income, part-time and full-time (about 60 per cent). Nearly half of mothers whose youngest child is under 4 also go out to work (ST, 1995, 66). The work that women do is changing rapidly. It used often to be part-time manual labour but now men are more in manual work, managerial posts, operating plant, machinery and vehicles, while women are more in clerical, secretarial, service and sales. There is now not too much difference in professional and technical levels of man–woman employment with the educational equality of the two sexes (or recent indications that girls are more strongly committed to education than boys). Still wives are much more fully involved in part-time work than husbands.

Many studies have shown a repeated pattern in relation to this trend. Men go out to work and expect to come home to leisure, while women go out to work and come home to work. This statement will generate a wave of male protest, but there is substance to it. One estimate is that full-time male employees do 12.5 fewer hours housework and have 13.3 more hours free time than their women counterparts (ST, 1994, 130). British men often do the washing up, at least more so than Italian men, but their role in the home is passive and not organisational. They do what they are told, but the wife retains executive responsibility for the home. Fred puts on Johnny's shirt, but Mum has made sure that a clean shirt will be available. Men need space to do one thing at a time; women have to juggle. American men will do a barbecue, but few meals inside.

This is reflected in leisure activities. Men have more time for sport. Often this is justified in terms of keeping fit, but actually, of course, women live longer because they work and get better regular, lifetime exercise than men. Men also attend spectator sport in large numbers and slump in front of the television set, remembering when they could score goals. Girls and women read more magazines and books, and use libraries more. Women are more likely to be involved with voluntary organisations, and men are likely to suggest that some women's shopping is not essential. There are many reflections which husbands and wives offer on the topic of their partner's leisure activities, but behind this lies a more important issue. It is the stressed living especially of many *double working women*, women who are full time in paid and domestic work. There are many cases of depression, exhaustion, ill-health and relational stress which grow out of this situation. Normally, also the wives face alone what should be the shared guilt of inadequate child-care. Part of the problem is male domestic laziness. We don't pull our overweight.

But that is not all of the problem. Dual-career marriages occur between couples who are well educated and highly trained. This group has used its market power to increase its rates of pay and the rewards of the job. But employers have responded by seeking to get their value for money, and increasing pressure is put on the highly paid to overwork. The result is stressed, overworking husbands and wives. But the problem is larger still, because companies and employers are increasingly following the patterns of making very high demands of the young, partly to offset the exhaustion of the middle-aged, and partly to construct the pattern of high differentials in income. The result is that in the formative years of marriage and starting a family both husband and wife are often furiously busy. The Japanese pattern of demanding total corporate loyalty from employees has infiltrated the West. The result is a widespread pattern of overwork with costs in terms of the quality of relationships. The decline of union effectiveness has helped the trend. Thus at the end of the twentieth century, with labour-saving devices everywhere, a large number of husbands and wives face the problem of substantial overwork. Work, they are effectively told, must come first.

Now this is a problem of modern capitalism. In the nineteenth century workers were often exploited with long hours but now the idiom has changed and it is the well-paid who are pushed into working long hours. In the European Union where the Social Chapter limits the number of hours worked, this is better regulated. German male workers have a strong mode of about thirty-nine hours. In Britain about 35 per cent of male employees are working over forty-five hours a week. Employees who are well-trained and operate valuable technologies and capital equipment are pushed harder than they should be. This capitalism, too, especially in the retailing business, has been prepared to break the rest norm of Sunday, so that for many all seven days involve hustle and graft. The degrees to which this pressure is resisted vary, but in Britain over the last two decades, we have moved headlong into middle-class overwork and its damage to marriages is incalculable.

Partly, this is because of the relative power of the middle-aged and young. The middle-aged are often sitting on property, organisational power and high incomes, and they put intense pressure on the young to prove themselves and 'earn' high rates of pay. The work costs of setting up home, marriage and starting a family thus peak heavily in the twenties and put intense pressures on many double earners.

Poverty and marriage

The shape of the class system has changed radically over a number of decades. Previously, there was a majority working class, who had one wage-earner and was comprised of relatively poor families. Although there was a crisis of unemployment in the 1930s, welfare provisions and the decline of unemployment during the 1950s and 1960s meant that these families fared relatively well. Beginning in the 1960s a long process of *embourgeoisement* took place, which moved a larger proportion of better educated and trained workers into middle-class standards of living. The commitment to people as citizens upheld a principle of good standards of life for all of the population. In the early 1980s there was a rebellion against this pattern by enough of what was now a middle-class majority following Thatcher in Britain and Reagan in the United States. This political group withdrew from commitment to the needs of poorer groups in a search for higher incomes, reduced taxation and a more affluent consumer lifestyle.

Actually, this has only partially happened, partly because many middle-class families have incurred all the costs associated with family breakdown, and partly because of the emergence of a *new de-resourced class*, which is sometimes called, 'the underclass'. This group has lost resources in the Reagan/Thatcherite revolution. Housing, education, healthcare, transport, public utility, tax and benefit changes have drawn resources from them. For a number of years in Britain the lowest fifth in terms of income have been paying a higher proportion of their incomes in taxes than the highest fifth. This has occurred with a deliberate encouragement of high competition for work among this group to keep wages and inflation down. The result has been a substantial group which has been de-resourced in relation to marriage and family life. For there is a pattern which emerges from these economic circumstances which has already been seen in the States among poorer Black groups. When the post-school male cannot obtain a job and begin to build the resources for marriage and family life, he becomes marginalised. Drugs, crime and violence build up. This de-resourced class is growing in size, and its costs in terms of non-work and welfare are now impoverishing the middle-class affluent groups who chose to ignore them. The deepest costs, however, are the loss of marital and family integrity among this group. What previous generations had fought painfully to build up has been thrown away in a generation. Another of the costs comes from resourcing a crime wave. Early pregnancy, poor fathering, inadequate housing and poor relational and parenting skills are growing rapidly among this group in many Western countries. It is an evil produced by unjust economic policies (Edelman, 1987; Holman, 1988; Madge, 1983).

Work and home

Work is in deep crisis in our present culture. The point about work is to do something which is good, useful and of service to others. Work should be communal, so that people work together and for one another. Technically, we have the equipment to make much work far easier. Yet today work is becoming more competitive, frenetic and individualised. Often people are working for their own career, what they are paid is more important than what they do, and they are caught in organisational time pressures which treat them as pawns. Given the massive influx of women to the workforce and the fact that men are hardly working shorter hours, it is likely that we are working substantially more than we have at other periods, outside wartime. This is an astonishing situation. We believe that we are much more efficient, but actually we are now having to work harder. Why is this? Actually, of course, there are deep inefficiencies in the approach to and organisation of work. Often we are producing bad, addictive products, which generate other costs in the system. The economic costs of family breakdown are considerable but we also demand, by choice, a more complex and affluent lifestyle. There is a deep interlocking in the pressure of work, often on both partners in a marriage, and the demands of consumption which their lifestyle generates.

Both are bad for marriage. The work pressures are complex, but their end result is often a loss of *shalom*, of peacefulness. Work imposed by the employer cannot be left any more. It follows him or her, claiming loyalty, worry and priority. It is a god claiming devotion and service. The words of Jesus cut into this pressured world and burst the bubble: 'Come to me, all of you who are weary and burdened, and I will give you rest. Take my yoke upon you and learn from me, for I am gentle and humble in heart, and you will find rest for your souls. For my yoke is easy and my burden is light' (Matt. 11: 28–30). This dethroning of the economism, the materialism is necessary if we are to be really free. Our whole attitude to work needs to change on a personal and societal level, so that people can live before God rather than serving Mammon but the change is also needed within marriages. The consumption and things do not matter: the relationship does.

13
MARRIAGE AND HOME LIFE

Where couples live

Marriages are deeply associated with homes. Marriage is a relationship, but it is an intimate one and throughout history the intimacies of daily life have taken place in and around a home. For a home allows a couple to be together, to share sexual union and privacy, to do the work and talking which form a marriage. We need to define some key features of home life and its relationship to marriage.

One is location. A home can be *matrilocal* – located close to the family of the wife – or *patrilocal* – near that of the husband – or *neolocal* – established in a new location. Actually in the West there is quite a variety of responses to this one issue. Many career-orientated families move to a new location for work and move quite frequently thereafter. One aspect of many Western marriages is the loss of immediate contact with parents which results. This occurs much less in traditional society, where marriages remain embedded much more firmly in the families of origin. Family contacts still remain very important in the West, but the underlying pattern of marital life is neolocal. This is what we normally understand by *the nuclear family*; it is the unit which is independent of the kinship networks of parents. It stands on its own.

This situation needs some thought. A man leaves his father and mother and cleaves to his wife, but in what sense does he leave? It should be a step of maturity and independence, but it is not necessarily geographical departure. In fact what happens in a lot of Western marriages is that couples experience degrees of bereavement which emerge from their new marriage. The break may have occurred earlier – at college, with the first job away, but often with marriage it becomes more pronounced. Husband and wife to an extent lose their father and mother. In all likelihood some post-marital depression is associated with this loss, especially if a partner sees marriage as a way of taking the spouse from his or her parents-in-law.

But moving the location of home raises other issues. It normally means levels of isolation, from friends, extended family, colleagues and neighbours. Unless couples acknowledge and face the levels of loss involved, they are likely not to understand their own moods and difficulties. Moving home is very difficult. Sometimes a couple does not make the decision together. His promotion means that they 'must' move and she is dragged away from friends and neighbours. However, the marriage is more important than the job, and a couple should decide together, without pressure, whether they move. There is another side to it, too. Home is the place where a couple are together, but it is less important than the marriage. If a partner is so completely tied to the house that it dominates decisions, there is another problem. Instead of the home being a place *for* the marriage, it becomes a place which takes priority *over* the marriage, with damaging consequences.

Making a home

Marriage involves homemaking. There is a dynamic to it which is vitally important because a home expresses the way a couple mean to live; it is designed, however limited the resources which are to be used. If a home has no books, people will not read. If it has no television set, they will not watch it. Couples continually solve problems of tidyness, cleaning, space utilisation, furnishing and decorating in their home. The dynamics of this process are very important in many marriages. Often the man is used to his mother and then his wife tidying up, and he regards it as his prerogative to drop whatever he wants wherever he wants and presume that it will be magically cleared. Sometimes the number of things which a couple has will not fit the space, and frustration is continually generated. His view of home and hers may be very different, and be reflected in the decoration of different rooms. The house may even be territorially owned – his space and her space. Sometimes he may retreat to, or be banished to, the shed at the bottom of the garden. There was an old pattern where the wife regarded the home as her territory, cleaned and controlled, and when he came home he came under *her* authority. He had to take his shoes off at the door and never leave the towel dirty. This is largely obsolete, but other variations follow. It is easy for the man to regard home as a place of comfort and rest, while for the woman it is a place of work. Or the wife who has worked for him all day can want him to work in return when he comes home doing DIY or other tasks. When these kinds of dynamics are going on a couple needs to consider the motives, resentments and control which are being exercised.

It is easy in our consumer culture for homemaking to be a dominating process. So much effort is pumped into the activity that couples have very little time for their relationship. The business of sharing, chatting, learning together, friendship and family contact becomes swamped in the process of setting up home, expanding it, and developing it further as a kind of personal territory. This is especially expressed in the idiom of the *ideal home*. This is such a powerful trend that we need to understand what drives it. The Ideal Home Exhibition, countless magazines, advertisements and consumer products push it avidly. The understanding is that when everything in the home is absolutely perfect, then the relationship will be. We are all given visions of homes that are peaceful, neat, warm and happy, which will make our marriages the same. Billions of pounds are being poured into this hope. It is literally driving the economies of the West, but it is a lie; it does not work.

First, in order to get the money necessary for this kind of lifestyle, many are finding ways of boosting their income at the expense of the poor; so it is an attitude which condones injustice and ignores the plight of others. This attitude is breaking down community, and the inequalities are generating patterns of burglary and insecurity which are increasingly making these ideal homes fortresses. The point is not just that people are fearful in their homes, but that this individualism is breaking down trust and creating patterns of isolation and loneliness which typify these magnificent homes. The rich man is still in his castle, but now he doesn't even have servants.

Second, these kinds of home require overwork. The great conclusion of the last few decades must be that with improved technology and productivity we have not bought more leisure, but only more elaborate lives. Full-time employees in Britain are working longer average hours than twenty years ago. Often husband *and* wife are overworking. This produces a most peculiar outcome. Affluent houses throughout the West are often largely unoccupied. Couples are out to work, often with long commuting times. They have several holidays away, and the result is that many of these houses in which so much time and effort is invested stand empty for much of the time. In contrast, the houses of the poor are overoccupied with unemployed people who cannot afford to go out. Such is the madness of our world.

Third, the whole promise is just a myth. The quality of our relationship depends directly on the love, patience, tenderness and companionship which they reflect. A new kitchen cannot sort out a temper. Redecorating the bedroom will not help a person who feels sexually used. There are great marriages in modest homes and lousy and disgusting marriages in great houses. Husbands and wives can quarrel on an Adam staircase and children can be petulant in a bath with gold-plated taps. The process of transference whereby the quality of the marriage comes from the home rather than the quality of the relationship is a stupid mistake, there is no substitute for loving one another.

Moving house

This is often quite stressful. It involves loss of friends, perhaps family, and a range of significant places. Yet it happens frequently. Many people have moved more than twenty times in their lives, and others are moving every year or two for much of their early marriage. Many employers require workers to move. A Glasgow police family had to do it once on Christmas Eve. The assumption is often made, as in Tebbit's, 'Get on your bike' remark that people should move to work, rather than work to people. The result is that some couples live as nomads, except that nobody travels with them, they flit from community to community and live in areas which are perpetually mobile.

The cost has often been greater to the wife. Women, especially those involved in full-time childcare often build networks of support and friendship. If these are ruptured, it hurts, and they are not easily replaced. The traditional breadwinner had a ready-made network of colleagues, although the new person at work often faced forms of intimidation and bullying. A high proportion of couples are therefore trying to generate new sets of friends and even new 'relatives' in new homes. Sometimes market pressures and speculation add to the mobility.

Public and private

Another great aspect of home life is the public/private split. This is an idiom which grows out of external moral control. Often people are invited to put on a front. They are to be respectable, dress up and behave well in front of other people. The assumption is that the disapproval of the public will be a motivation for controlling bad behaviour. It is interesting to see children exploiting this pattern. They learn that they can behave badly or demand sweets in public, because their parents will not smack them in public the way they would at home. The idea of public respectability, however, has as its flipside the view that domestic behaviour, what is private, has no moral control. Sadly, there is substantial weight to this view. *Marital abuse* and *violence* often happen in private and are accompanied by processes of hiding. Both aggressor and victim often hide what goes on. Crucial in such situations, if separation does not occur, is making sure that a good number of people know about and will address any recurrence. Rowing and verbal abuse often happen privately in ways which do not occur publicly. This signals that external respect is the motive for restraint. It is a weak one and if a dual standard emerges of public and private behaviour, the person concerned loses all sense of personal integrity and is seen as a hypocrite by the partner. Sometimes the impossibility of arguing or confronting a public figure – a boss, teacher or employer – means that the person scapegoats his/her partner in private, like kicking the dog rather than the traffic warden. Sometimes sexual unfaithfulness which is undetected is seen as acceptable.

A biblical understanding cuts across this. God looks at the heart and does not deal in appearances. Jesus made it clear that 'there is nothing hidden which will not be revealed' (Matt. 10:26) and upbraided the Pharisees who were keen on outside appearance while underneath there were attitudes of murder, status and exploitation. Social fear and conformity are not meant to be the motivation for good behaviour. It must just be good before God. Jesus called his disciples to live transparently; what is whispered in the ear will be proclaimed in the supermarket and what is done in the dark will be seen on television. Before God there is no private and public. We shall know ourselves as God knows us.

At the same time there is privacy to marriage. It consists just of boundaries which allow the marriage to be the full exclusive relationship it is meant to be. It was entirely consistent in biblical times with a whole family being in one bed. It has nothing to do with hiding evil, nor does it require guard dogs, curtains and a gun behind the door. In fact it has little to do with the Western constructs of privacy which are now so dominant. These often mean that parents and friends do not know if a couple has problems or joys, that little is shared, and the insights of one generation are not available to the next. Sometimes marriages develop with private emotions, problems and traumas which could easily evaporate, if shared.

Marriage as consumption

The changing meaning of the home is largely dictated by consumption. It is an incredibly powerful modern cultural idiom. Actually, the home is an important place for production – of food, children, workers, education, relationships, wisdom, care, refreshment and energy. Any good economy of the household would identify the contributions made by the household to the economy, because they are crucial. Nevertheless the myth exists that homes are places of consumption. Everything which is produced disappears down the black hole of domestic consumption (Tiemstra *et al.*, 1990, 133–66). The home, through television and advertising is a point of tremendous need generation (Walter, 1985). Thus couples come to see the home, their place, as a consumption-driven location. The motives which shape this consumption vary. Sometimes it is security, hedonism, comfort, entertainment or the need to collect. It may be image, fashion or creating an ideal home. Expressing love in relationships through things is a powerful motive, as we rediscover each Christmas. A belief in quality, aesthetics or a beautiful environment may drive consumption. Or it may feel subjective needs, impulses, ambitions and hopes (Storkey, 1993, 207–16; Shields, 1992). The norm of a high income, high consumption lifestyle drives much of life and marriage.

Consumption not only costs time to earn the money, but it is also itself time-expensive. Shopping itself takes time; it is second only to television as a leisure activity. Goods themselves demand time. A person has a yacht which he may use for two weeks in a year and yet spend one week in transporting and servicing. A coffee jar is replaced by a grinder, filters and a percolator, all of which need cleaning and which take more time to use. The space used for domestic equipment in turn generates extra kitchen requirements, and so on. Thus, many homes absorb money, energy, commitment and time, while people have less time to spend on them. They dominate the marriage relationship. They channel domestic time away from chat, sharing, hearing one another. They replicate the demands and noise of a consumer society and destroy the peace which a marriage relationship requires.

THE STAGES OF MARRIAGE

Marriage as a walk of faith

Often marriage is viewed as a *state*. People are supposed to get married and live happily ever after. Actually, of course, it is locked into the drama of life and for many of us comprises many of the *stages* through which we develop. Each of these has its own dynamic and raises its own issues. In this chapter we shall examine some of these stages and the kinds of issues which arise in each one. Really, there is a pattern of development which occurs which is continually changing, and hopefully developing. However, this is not always the pattern. Often, if some aspect of the marital relationship is wrong, or the marriage becomes wrongly directed, it can face patterns of setback and frustration which may last a decade or more. A Christian understanding is that marriage, like all aspects of our personal lives can be redeemed into ways that are blessed again. Thus, marriages can always be good.

There is another element here in this Christian understanding. Often the approach to marriage is competitive. My marriage can only be good if another one is bad. If we are rich, and they are not, then we have a good marriage. Individuals often seek the best partners and may feel that they have got the second best. This competitive notion is completely wrong. A marriage is as good as the relationship itself, and it is possible for all marriages to be good, or at least a lot better, if they are shaped by love and an openness to God. Whoever we are, if we are really open to God's Spirit and die to self, amazing changes can follow. What then are the challenges of marriage?

The newly-wed couple

There are a number of decisions which are made at marriage.

- The decision to marry must be made well. If it has not been, then the space must be made for it to happen without pressure.
- The decision about paid and unpaid work within the marriage needs to be made together. The central reality is that each partner's work must be equally honoured and that each must be willing to give to and serve the other.
- The choice about where to live needs to be made together. Her home, his home, friends, work are part of the picture, but it is easy for one person's priorities to automatically dominate.
- The quality of a marriage depends basically on how fully a couple learns from Jesus and the Scriptures. A marriage needs to find ways of feeding biblical truths into the relationship.
- A couple needs to share friends and family. This requires that her friends become his and vice versa, but also that the friendships do not intrude into the marriage in ways which interfere with its intimacy. Her parents are now his, and they should have the respect and honour of his own parents. The only point about the weakness of our parents is that we should learn from them.
- The husband may well be lazy and not understand how to do a lot of household tasks. He must be prepared to learn quickly and pull his weight.
- Marriage is often a time of loss – partial loss of family, home, friends, perhaps job, especially for the woman, and these sorrows need to be recognised and shared. Sharing sorrow is important.
- With marriage comes a decision about the kind of depth

and level of sharing which will occur in the relationship. Central is the view of the world and faith. If these are different and not Christian, there may well be underlying problems built into the relationship which will continue for years. Basically, a relationship is as deep as the relationship which the couple has with God. Here start patterns of conversation, prayer and sharing which will develop in the future. Television is the biggest danger to the quality of the relationship.

- A couple when they first marry will think individualistically and have to learn to bond and think together. Pressure on one another to conform is a weak way of doing it. Far better is mutual submission – really opening ourselves to our partner's point of view and concerns.

- It is easy at this stage for one partner's agenda to dominate in areas like where the couple lives, what work they do and what lifestyle they adopt. The partner who tends to be dominant especially needs to think themselves into mutual decision-making where the work and needs of each are equally valued.

- A couple will also make fundamental decisions about where their egos are. His or hers could dominate, or both can be submitted to the will and purposes of God. 'Thy will be done' as a commitment to God is a good basis for small egos and harmony.

- Attitude problems which are wrong – blaming, being self-opinionated, self-righteous, self-pitying, selfish and proud become exposed fairly quickly. They can be shared as problems to be solved together with prayer and self-awareness.

- Couples will be surprised how, after their single life, issues from their own family background which have been dormant for years will suddenly jump up and hit them. They often will not know what is going on in them or their partner. It is important not to *transfer* problems from the previous generation into this one, and it often needs a great deal of careful sharing and counselling not to do so.

Sometimes the wife faces a big transition at marriage. In more traditional families the husband continues working, while she moves home, changes her network of friends and moves into looking after this man.

Early family life

The transition to having a family is not made by some couples, around 10 per cent. This situation may cause sorrow and yearning, or be made by choice, or be more circumstantial, but it should be shared, without blame of either self or partner. For the integrity of the marriage remains, and although having children is a blessing, God gives many other kinds of blessing in life. For those with children it must be put in perspective, even though it seems quite all-consuming at the time.

- Pregnancy is a time of glory for the woman, even when she is being sick! She should not fear the loss of her figure or fear being 'trapped' in motherhood and so view the birth negatively, but love and enjoy the baby into birth.
- Father and Mother should share pregnancy and birth together. The fully committed sharing of the Father in childcare and in loving his wife unreservedly is essential. For quite a while he will be her servant.
- Sometimes men feel sexually alienated during pregnancy and childbirth. This is *their* problem. They have caused the pregnancy and should emotionally share and fully engage with the whole process of pregnancy, birth and babycare. It is a glorious process. Watching babies is far better than television.
- Parents do not own or possess children, but are given them by God to look after and love. They cannot really

be proud of them, because God did all the creative stuff. Basically parents are alongside children before God and should never dominate or be self-focused.

- A mother, and a father, may be socially isolated during the early years of the children. Often there is a need for help with parenting, and others especially older people and families should be asked. Companionship for one another, and with others, matters during this time.

- Babies and children are deeply affected by moods. A home should be shaped by the steady joy of the parents, not by parental reactions to babies and children. Patience and self-control matter. Rows are often about trivia and can usually be avoided if a couple ask one another for help.

- It is easy for worry to build up. It should be shared and prayed about. Wherever possible the cause of the worry should be tackled. Jesus tells us not to let anxiety build up; we can't control life, but just have to live it day by day trusting God.

- The marriage relationship does not dissolve into family, but a couple should retain the intimacy and closeness of the union throughout and not allow patterns of alienation to build up.

- There is often intense pressure on young couples to overwork. Many employers in Britain give scant regard to family responsibilities. Constant stress is no virtue. This pressure must be faced. It is usually much better to be poor than not to be able to look after your chidlren or share life as a couple.

Early midlife

The dynamic of marriage is often faster than we recognise. We change rapidly with the challenges and issues of life. That change should be marked by the steadiness and obedience of Christian faith. A marriage should be steady and drenched in love, so that each partner is *for* the other. And there should be a growth in maturity because couples continually develop in their relationship with God. But other things often happen too.

- Failure is a fairly common experience in personal terms, work and family life. It can become routine and defeating. It can be made by a partner into the dominating characteristic of the relationship: 'I live with a failure'. Many things are not failures that seem so. We can learn from our failures and start again with forgiveness and insight. Couples can share failure.
- Fatigue often damages marriage and family life. Much of it is self-induced and can be rectified – early nights, good exercise, disciplined work, little alcohol and no overeating. God has given us work and rest, and you can't cheat on either.
- Married couples always underestimate the fear that each can induce in the other by criticism, anger, and withholding love. Fear leads to withdrawal which is also a weak response.
- A couple must always sort out their differences *with each other*, never through their children or anyone else. That just leaves children with problems which are insoluble, at least until the children understand their parents' weaknesses.
- A couple should share all they do, even if they do it separately, by talking, prayer and support. Nothing should be done which is an expression of breaking away from the partner. There should be togetherness, co-operation and freedom, probably in that order.
- It is easy for ideals like Career. the Ideal Home, Sport, Affluence, Education and Reputation to dominate home life. They are false and destructive, and they need to be firmly put in their place. Living a life of regret, 'if only', is debilitating and undermines the life God has given us.
- Moving involves far more than a job. A couple and possibly their children should make the decision to, or not

to, together. It often involves leaving friends, neighbours, family and the husband especially should never underestimate the change.

- Parents educate children. All the really formative education comes from Mum and Dad, directly through teaching and also through the way they live. Time with children, educating them, is a basic need and what they are taught by the way their parents *live*, they will learn.
- It is always easier to teach children, by example and through the Bible, what good living is, than to try to correct them later.
- Children's direct relationship with God should always be acknowledged, encouraged and given space within the family dynamics. Children should and can grow up knowing and loving God as their father.
- There is a danger of work pressure on the wife. She may be doing paid work, housework and family care, while he does paid work and relaxes. There needs to be a full sharing of work and engagement in family relationships, not passive fathering.
- Parents tend to think of themselves, their time, their interests and work as more important than their children's concerns. There should be no status in a family. Everybody is equally important, and the family should not be child-centred either.
- Love is not reactive, and it should grow with self-knowledge and the knowledge of the partner. There is always more to discover about the partner, and someone who is bored or dissatisfied reflects the way they have closed their own minds or emotions.

Later midlife

Now children are older and the marriage relationship has developed through a number of years. The meaning of the marriage relationship and the kind of love it involves will be evident, and how the children are brought up will be strongly shaped.

- Problems which have been around for a long time unaddressed may now become chronic for the other partner – poor communication, lack of care, irritation, laziness, poor sex. The subject may be so used to being like that that (s)he cannot see a problem.
- There may be new areas of life – faith, leisure, work, parenting, friendship – which a couple does not share. Mutuality is a continual development.
- Couples will face the issue of the freedom and maturity of the children. Control will bring reaction and rebellion. Any rivalry between parents and children will be destructive. What the children are like may reflect the failings of the parents.
- If a couple is committed to ideals of being young in appearance, body, attitudes and self-image, aging will be a crisis. If they are not, it probably won't be.
- The possible growing dependency of grandparents begins to be an issue.
- If husband and wife are both involved in work quite fulltime, the caring role in family life may be neglected. Careers can become very demanding at this stage and have important lifestyle implications.
- Emotions like regret, guilt, long-term anger and depression and cynicism, which look back negatively can settle on one or both partners in ways which are not constructive. Reflection, forgiveness, sadness and real remorse faced with God can be healing and strengthening.
- Aloneness may occur much more, from children, spouse and others. It can be a shock, or can be shared with God in a way which makes it rich and formative.
- This is a time when events, experience, thought and understanding may challenge the world view and philosophy of each partner. Simple answers like materialism, success and the quest for happiness will probably drop

away. A world-view crisis can be very complex for a couple to face. They need good communication. Sharing Christian insights and travelling a common road of faith are important.

● Earlier character traits may drop away and change. The activist, joking, power-seeking, happy, accommodating or serene person may be so no longer. This requires careful marital listening.

● Some patterns of conflict, blame, anger and withdrawal will be so deep and engrained that couples expect not to solve them, when actually they could be opened up and tackled, especially with time to talk and listen carefully. Sharing can go on and on to depths we do not yet know and love can re-emerge and grow.

Old age

Couples often now have a considerable time together in old age, twenty years or more. Sometimes illness and death create difficulties and sadness, or people are not what they were. But often a lot of the trivia of marriage drops away and the faithfulness and love come to full fruition.

● Retirement usually means the husband coming back to be at home after the wife. If he is entering her domain, or he takes over there will be problems. New areas of sharing need to be rediscovered.

● As death approaches, the meaning of life seems especially crucial. Each partner and preferably both together need the space to tend to their relationship with God.

● The loss of those with shared experience and awareness means that older couples will often not be understood. The loss of real communication across the generations reflects our impoverishment.

● Couples become dependent on one another through illness and infirmity. If there has been a good pattern of sharing and mutuality, this will be natural. Physical limitations need not matter too much.

- The freedom from work and other responsibilities may give a couple great freedom to take up new challenges and opportunities. If these are self-centred, they may be less rewarding. This can be a continuation of 'laying up treasure in heaven' time, when a couple does only what is good, without external pressures from employers and others.
- A need for security, and other fears, may arise out of the relative weakness of old age. Anxieties can grow in later years, or they can be committed to God and removed.
- The death of others, and especially a spouse, involves sadness and mourning, which reflects the goodness and character of the person. It is especially difficult when there are unresolved problems, regret or anger. These are best faced earlier and dealt with in relation to God. We always submit one another to God.

LAW AND MARRIAGE

Law as an aspect of marriage

We have already established that it is not the law which makes a marriage centrally what it is, but the inner troth relationship between the couple in conformity with God's law and purposes for marriage. The wedding service recognises and affirms this reality, but the law establishes the issues of justice which occur in relation to a marriage – how each partner should rightly treat one another and how the rest of society should respect and honour the marriage. The law is therefore a public statement about what is right in and for marriage; it defines the public norms for marital living. In Judaeo-Christian terms it has a depth which is often ignored. In Moses' words,

> The Lord your God commands you this day to follow these decrees and laws; carefully observe them with all your heart and with all your soul. You have declared this day that the Lord is your God and that you will walk in his ways, that you will keep his decrees, commands and laws, and that you will obey him.
>
> (Deut. 26:16–17)

The law in this deeper sense is the guide to life, and especially it is the way one lives justly and righteously, not doing wrong to one's neighbour. The State is meant to construct a legal framework in submission to what is just and good in this and other human relationships.

Sadly, in the case of marriage law we are looking at a

mess. For many centuries the laws, established by men, majored on a view of wives as the property of the husband, following patriarchal Roman forms. Then, in addition, marriage was seen as a private matter largely outside the scope of the law. Further, because marriage was mainly understood in terms of the church wedding, there was a distinct failure to develop the legal understanding of marriage. In addition, because the rich usually had recourse to marriage and divorce law, its focus was mainly on property. The legal profession has also been much more interested in defending its clients and earning fees than in clarifying principles of marital justice. And finally, there occurred a disjunction between marriage and divorce law which we shall investigate shortly.

However, an additional problem occurred through the approaches taken to marriage and divorce law. Many of the attitudes were just traditional, depending on previous case law, or positive, seeing the law as building up a corpus of judgements on the basis of responding to particular cases. But the overwhelming philosophy behind this area of law for the last hundred years or more has been liberal individualism. It has passed through a number of stages. First, the rights of partners have been stressed within what is understood as a contractual view of marriage. But as the perceived terms of the contract have loosened, the rights have gradually become diluted. At the end of the twentieth century this trend has finally issued in a view that marriage can be arbitrarily broken on terms of no-fault divorce. Let us examine this process in greater detail.

Liberal divorce law today

There are a number of trends which have contributed to the situation at the end of the twentieth century.

1. Marriage law and divorce law

Over the last few decades there has been an increasing gap between marriage law and divorce law. It is not clear what marriage law means, for although the married state has been the basis for a whole range of maritally related legislation, *marriage law* as such does not really exist. The Church of England wedding service or the registry office marriage are legal commitments, but not legally expressed. Earlier divorce law saw marital offences as culpable, but especially since the 1973 Matrimonial Causes Act there has been a retreat from this position. The proposed reform, accepting marriage as irretrievably broken without culpability, sits across a gap from the promise to 'forsake all others' and to marry for life. Divorce law is out of touch with the commitments made at marriage, and Divorce Law Reform does not intend to address the issue.

2. Justice within marriage

There has been relatively little concern about justice within marriage down the centuries. This is probably because most of those offended against were women and the male defendants and judges were able to keep the issues from having damaging exposure. The liberal trend, followed in Mackay's Divorce Law Reform has been to marginalise questions of justice within marriage. In its desire to escape from blaming between the partners, and to avoid the complexities of judgements within marriage, it moves to adopting a *no fault* approach universally to divorce. The problem is that marriage does involve important mutual obligations, and some partners do offend against these, leaving their spouse hurt, damaged, economically exploited and abused. Indeed, it may well be the case that in half or three-quarters of marriages one partner feels, perhaps with good cause, that he or she has been substantially wronged. Desertion, cruelty and violence, adultery and unreasonable behaviour are substantial wrongs. Sometimes the idea that marriages 'just break down' is taken as the universal type for divorce. No fault divorce tends to that view. But it is undeniable that in a substantial number of cases one partner has high responsibility, and the other partner and children suffer. This is important because removing responsibility from law degrades public and private standards of living.

3. The problem of a single state law

Matrimonial law is already becoming problematic because cohabitation exists alongside marriage. How much legislation governing marriage should be extended to cohabitees is an open question, partly because cohabitees may define their relationship in terms other than that of marriage. Over the last few decades divorce law has changed in accord with a specific cultural view. It sees marriage as a relationship which should be terminated when a partner finds the relationship permanently unsatisfactory. This view has been represented in law. Another view, which may be held by, say, 20–60 per cent of the adult population, is that marriage is for life and partners should not think in individual terms about what is a union. It is a view which is held by many moral and religious groups. It has been under cultural attack for a number of decades from a variety of individualist views, but none could contest its importance. It is unrepresented in law.

4. Pluralism and the law

A very important aspect of law involves the recognition of differences of view and approach which are nevertheless recognised as being impartially subject to law. Thus, the law of contract does not say what a contract should be, but defines how it should be accepted in law in whatever terms it might be stated. In fact, most institutions – companies, charities, unions, political parties, schools and universities are approached this way. They define themselves and the law codifies some general principles around and incorporating their self-defined existence. There are, for example, a variety of forms of company incorporation.

It could be argued that this is actually part of the democratic principle – that institutions and organisations be allowed to define themselves, and that law then incorporates this pluralism into its statutes. Clearly, there are overriding principles of justice which prevent any such group from being a law unto itself, but standardisation is less of a legal principle than is sometimes thought to be the case. We could conclude that democratic principles should allow the expression of all important views of marriage and divorce in law, but that at present only the liberal view is represented by the State.

5. Legalism is perceived as a problem

There is a perception that law tends to create complications in divorce proceedings, while mediation would be far better. There are a number of interpretations of this move. Its focus may be to cut legal expense. Legal Aid in matrimony and family proceedings is heading towards £400 million. By paying mediators much lower rates than lawyers this figure may be cut and that is certainly the aim in the Mackay proposals (Mackay, 1995, 42). Another implied criticism may be that solicitors by acting for their client and seeking to maximise work and income, generate confrontation. The legal profession would argue that clients have needed, and will still need, protection of their rights. A third reason given is that the aim is to counsel divorcees about the process they are going through. The hope is that some will pull back from divorce and others will work through the process with more mutuality. This third element is quite an important new departure. It recognises that the legal process involves and is related to personal and relational issues which cannot be handled in a court. It may be, however, that those who have legal and financial obligations look for reforms which will lessen them.

6. The Churches are confused by the existing State–Church relationship

The position of the Church of England was set, I believe wrongly, by the report, *Putting Asunder* (Church of England). It concluded that the State should follow the path of recognising that marriages broke down, and that this fact should shape divorce law reform, largely moving away from rigid culpability. Its internal discipline did not allow the remarriages of divorcees in church, irrespective of the question of whether they were initiators or victims of the divorce. Recently this provision has been made more discretionary.

But the outcome of this initial espousal, as the National Church, of the trend towards liberal no-fault divorce is that the Church of England and other churches have tended to accept changes which actually disagree with their own explicit views of marriage. There are a variety of forms of casuistry which validate this process, but they are not really convincing. Consequently, the churches at present are locked into a contradictory stance, affirming, albeit equivocally, one view of marriage while accepting a completely different dynamic behind divorce reform. Either you believe in lifelong marriage in life and in law, or you do not.

7. The 1973 Matrimonial Causes Act has effectively been subverted

When an Act has been passed it does not always operate as was intended. The overall rubric of the Act was irretrievable breakdown, but it included two kinds of agenda. The first three cases were of behaviour that the petitioner was deeming as culpable – adultery, unreasonable behaviour and desertion (for two years) and bringing as grounds for divorce. The last two were evidence of *de facto* breakdown

– two years separation if both parties agreed or five years if they disagreed. This was evidence of irretrievable breakdown. The intent of the Act was to move away from the more culpable grounds to the evidence of breakdown, but it did not work.

The reason was that lawyers exploited the special procedure rules which were introduced in 1973 and extended to uncontested cases in 1977. These allowed uncontested cases presented under the adultery and unreasonable behaviour heads, if they were not contested, to go through in a matter of months. Some 75 per cent of cases are handled under this head and they go through in an average time of six months. What is going on here? I do not have hard evidence, but suggest the normal practice is for the partner who has left his or her spouse, often for another relationship, to put pressure on the other partner to go through with an uncontested, culpable divorce. The divorce can take place quickly, or it will drag on for two or even five years. Some cohabit while separated but still married and commit effective bigamy. But many who have been deserted trade the uncontested divorce for reasonable terms of settlement. Usually the respondent is male.

The present reforms seem deeply inadequate. They merely continue a liberal trend and build in all the principles of irresponsibility and defeat which are part of the process. What may be needed is a different view of the whole process. What is suggested below is an alternative form of marriage and divorce law, which could be optional for couples who chose it. It, or some variant, would allow a stronger form of legal commitment to embody their choice. Its central view of marriage would be as a life-long partnership, and divorce would be seen more fully in that light, rather than as irretrievable breakdown. Its intend would be to develop the strength and stability of marriage, and it could have the effective support of the Christian churches and other religious and counselling groups. It could be structured something as follows.

A marriage and divorce law

Marriage is based on a procedure of Registration, First Signing and Wedding signing. The *Registration*, which normally follows engagement, is a notification which sets in procedure the following: The couple will discuss together, perhaps also with counsellor, mature friend and parents the following areas.

1. Their parents' attitudes to marriage and each other, and especially any breakdown of the parental marriage.
2. Previous sexual relationships and exclusive friendships.
3. Any drug, alcohol or other addictive patterns in past or family.
4. Religious attitudes and values.
5. Any personal or family tendencies to violence or aggression.
6. The history of their childhood and teenage years.
7. Any important experiences of joy, sorrow or trauma.
8. Any fears, needs or personal weaknesses.
9. Sexual attitudes and values.
10. Attitudes to family and children.
11. Attitudes to education, work and money.
12. Levels of honesty and self-awareness.
13. Their relationships with friends and family members.

The point of these discussions is not to create an inquisition, but that there should be a good basis of personal sharing and that the choice to marry should be made with open eyes. Similarly, if problems arise, the point may not be to clear them up fully before the wedding (although some might need to be fully sorted out), but for the couple to be sure that they have the basis for addressing them together. It is possible for Marriage Preparation Classes and other forms of marriage preparation to be contributed here by Churches and other voluntary organisations.

When the registration stage is completed, according to the couple's satisfaction, they move forward to the *First Signing*. At the First Signing each partner would commit themselves by signature to the following. They declare that they intend to marry their partner assenting to the following statements, which constitute the MARRIAGE BOND.

1. I love my partner (name) as I love myself, unconditionally.
2. I am committed to my partner for life.
3. I enter into a full marital union retaining no areas of private life.
4. I am committed to a full sexual relationship with my partner which is tender and exclusive. Adultery and other forms of personal unfaithfulness I rule out.
5. I will not use violence or intimidation within my marriage.
6. I will avoid addiction to drugs, alcohol or any other dangerous compulsions.
7. I am committed to respect and honour my partner, and not to dominate or misrepresent them.
8. I will share my energy, work, income, property and other economic resources unreservedly with my partner.
9. I agree to tackle serious marital problems honestly by discussion and counselling, with a commitment to mutuality.
10. I choose never to transfer, even in part, the commitment I have to marital union with my partner, to another person.
11. I am committed to sharing the parenting of the children we have, to work at agreed parenting, and to fully respect my partner as parent.
12. I accept that the depth of my union and commitment to my partner goes beyond legal requirements or merely fulfilling these conditions.

The first signing will be followed by a period of two months or more, which constitutes a period of reflection where each partner assesses further whether they are able to go forward to marriage on these terms. It is to be noted that the marriage bond is not a contract in the traditional sense of the word, because in a contract each party retains their individual status, whereas this marriage is a union. But it is a bond which has legal status. This is a commitment which each makes to the other in law.

The full commitment is made in the *Second Signing*. Here the couple drop intention and sign to these statements as the legal basis of their marriage. Obviously, any doubts which have emerged must be tackled before this second signing. Probably the second signing should occur before the wedding, so that it is not caught up in the celebration of the event and can be recognised as the voluntary legal basis to marriage which each party accepts. It would also include the supplementary legislation.

The Marriage Bond should stand as it is in the lives of the couple involved. It could be backed by supplementary legislation, to which the couple also commit themselves. This occurs at three levels, each hopefully used more sparingly – *Crisis, Separation* and *Divorce*.

Crisis is a procedure where when one partner declares that there is an issue which one partner decides cannot be addressed internally in a marriage, the other is required (or both, if they agree) to submit to a short course of counselling on that issue and to receive a report, copied to the spouse. The agency to which the partner submits is chosen at marriage or later and has no statutory role. It merely allows a couple to recognise that a crisis exists, for if it is there for one it is there for both. It also gives both partners an external assessment of the issue that concerns them. Hopefully churches and other agencies would train people for this kind of task.

Separation would be requested by the petitioner on the grounds of obvious culpable behaviour like violence, unreasonable behaviour and adultery. When granted by the courts, it would require the respondent to leave the marital home for six months or a year. Desertion would be treated as *de facto* separation and the same conditions would apply. At the end of the designated period, the petitioner says whether the separation is to end or continue.

Divorce occurs on the grounds of culpable offences which include adultery, desertion, and unreasonable behaviour. Here the already agreed result of divorce would be for the respondent to forfeit 60 per cent of marital assets and 50 per cent of the joint post-marital income for the next ten years. Adjustments would be made for child support. Divorce could also occur on the grounds of irretrievable breakdown, which requires three years of separation without cohabitation or sexual relationships with anyone else.

It could also be that *marital offence* be introduced, whereby a person who is responsible in some obvious way for breaking up a marriage be held culpable and required to pay, say, half a year's salary to the injured party. For a real offence has been committed which is at present ignored at law.

There is the possibility here that good marriage law would chase out bad, but it would at least concentrate people's minds to work out precisely what kind of relationship they intended to enter.

MARITAL BREAKDOWN
AND RECOVERY

Why do marriages break down?

Already we have uncovered a whole range of explanations
as to why marriages today might be failing; they explain the
crisis, our crisis, and here we bring them together. Our
concern is not to explain away and justify marital breakdown, because it is a process which is damaging beyond
words, but to uncover the lie. People are approaching their
marriage, themselves and their partner in terms which are
seriously flawed. There are mistakes being made which
could be rectified. Attitudes have been allowed to destroy
people and relationships which should be good and rich. I
have seen people who have been left by their partners or
who have experienced marital breakdown who are fine and
lovely people. In my judgement their partners are mad.
There is a process of failure or rejection which has gone on
which just should not happen. In a sense the British public
have had this drama played out before their eyes. The
Prince and Princess of Wales were, it was believed, the
nation's best. Without accepting any aristocratic nonsense
each had a lot to give. Yet we have seen a tragedy unfold,
no more important than the breakdown of any other marriage, but more public. Can these not be addressed? For, as
we have seen, there is no alternative to good marriages.
Good persons have to grow in good intimate relationships.

Already we must face *the great excuse*. It is that *marriage*,
or this marriage, is to blame, not the individuals within it.
This is the basic scapegoating move which allows many partners
to run. The good guy misunderstood by his wife or the woman

looking for more excitement have probably not looked at themselves, or their partner, properly. They have just quit, carrying their own problems tortoise-like on their backs.

It is important to understand the structure of this chapter. It will set out a whole range of reasons why marriages can break down. Some are more important than others. In the list below some are marked with an *, but others may be more important for a particular person. In some senses they are cumulative, in that carrying a lot of them is more burdensome. All of them can be tackled, but the process is not mechanical. Marriage is quite simply a union between a man and a woman, and when they love and respect one another, they can work and grow through these problems. But at the same time this process has basically to be one of Christian faith. There are certain points of reference which are basic to our existence and the meaning of marriage. A couple cannot properly be healed unless they grow into a knowledge of their worth before God, know that love and respect are both a command and are true to their partner. They need to face their wrongs, not worship themselves, repent and know forgiveness on God's terms of grace. Thus, these points call for a personal response. If they are relevant, they engage with us. At its simplest, being followers of Jesus Christ is the best way to heal a marriage.

Family of origin

1. Families where parents quarrel, blame, express anger and violence are difficult to shake off. They encourage attitudes of I am right and my will be done, and they require a spiritual change in adult life which espouses Christian patience, humility and peacefulness.

2. Families where children are criticised, attacked, told they are no good and ignored, lead to patterns of defensiveness and armour, which are difficult in a marriage. They can also lead to assertiveness and

counter-attack. These prevent problems being addressed. Submitting to the loving criticism of God, and a partner is a way through this. 'Neither do I condemn thee. Go and sin no more,' said Jesus.

3. Families where the parental marriage breaks down tell the child that marriages do not work. If they are the gender of the spouse that was left, marriage may be a source of fear and trauma. If they are the other gender they have to *leave* the irresponsibility and lack of love of that parent.

*4. Children who are left by a parent, or who experience being unloved, will often retain a deep yearning and hunger for parental love, which will remain the agenda in adult life. Sometimes blame is transferred to the spouse. Sometimes illness, concern with appearance and a devastating fear of being unloved will remain. The central answer is a recognition of God's love of each of us and commitment to who we are, a recognition of hurt and eventually forgiveness of parents.

5. Families where money management, drink, domestic order, management of time and compulsive TV watching are problems require the next generation to fight for something different.

6. Families where children are pressured to achieve, to be good, to succeed will often leave obsessive commitments rooted in the children into adulthood. They may be parental agendas for the adult child which carry over into the marriage, which need to be cut.

7. Family values like trust, co-operation, selfishness, competition, honesty, recrimination, irritability, hard work, care, aggression or tenderness will often deeply influence a person growing up among them. Where these are destructive, they will be very difficult to shake off. They can be fully faced and rejected.

*8. Poor communication is endemic in many families – at least at some levels. It is affected by noise, TV, poor listening, quarrelling, overwork and lack of time to share, closed minds, no-go areas, poor education and a lack of belief in talking and thinking. The communication of couples grows from the parental communication base. It can get stuck or continually develop.

9. Strong male–female segregation or opposition in a family, especially from macho men or untrusting women can easily be passed on. The Male sport, drinking, leisure and Female work model is disastrous. It needs fighting.

View of life

*1. If a person has a view of life which centres on him/herself, then relationships will be external. There will be little sense of empathy or sharing. My wants, needs, understanding, feelings will be central. Relational issues will tend to be viewed self-righteously, and there will be a tendency for the individual to use his/her partner as a means to gratification and happiness. Jesus's remedy was radical; *die to self*.

2. Many believe in an ideal partner, romantic love and an idealised view of marriage. Marriage on these terms will not work. The ideal/actual division leads many to engage in unreal quests for the ideal man or woman, or another kind of relationship, which prevents them seeing with respect the lovely partner they actually have.

3. Many view emotions of love and infatuation as a law unto themselves. It makes how they feel about a relationship, which is probably quite arbitrary, self-validating. Sometimes people feel neglected, angry, ignored and at other times infatuated and euphoric. But emotions seen this way are very unreliable, and they need to be grounded on a firmer base for living and feeling.

4. Some people are hedonistic and put their pleasure

now first. This can mean lack of forethought, and a partner being used and abused. The search for pleasure is basically vanity and only leads to disappointment. Real joy is God-given and only arises from what is good.

5. Those who believe in controlling life and therefore in controlling their partner undermine the ability of their spouse to love them freely.

6. Some people live existentially and see no possibility of long-term commitment. God's commitment to us is more than life-long and it is possible to learn the meaning of steadfast love for marriage.

7. What is often going on in marital problems is the crisis of one or other partner in relation to the great issues of life – relationship with God, relationship to the creation, personal identity, how we can know what is true, the meaning of justice, the problem of evil, the nature of love, what good living is, death and who Jesus is. Respect for one another's thinking and searching is important.

Sex

1. Premarital sex with other partners is dangerous, because it disconnects sex from faithfulness and complete sharing. It is easy for a person to retain an experimental or self-centred view of sex from previous relationships. This needs repentance and change.

2. The use of power and pressure to have sex, or the use of its withdrawal as power is destructive. 'Do not arouse or awaken love until it so desires' (S. of S. 8:4).

3. Pornography is demeaning to the partner and reduces sex to the gratification of lust. It should be absent from a marriage.

*4. Having sex when there is no shared sense of love is destructive, because the act should be an expression of that love. Otherwise it is hypocritical and false, and feels wrong.

*5. Adultery is always a fundamental repudiation and dishonouring of the partner. It is an expression that a marriage is effectively dead. Adultery with excuses is even worse. It is an absolute prohibition and can never be justified. The repentance required to reconstitute a marriage after it is often deeper than the offending partner recognises.

6. Loss of self-control, obsessive sex, performance sex and comparisons between people are all destructive.

7. Good sex needs time, rest and energy, sensitivity, trust, honesty and love, love, love of one another.

The marriage

1. Lack of equality may rule. Those who feel superior or inferior in terms of money, gender, education, culture, power, skills, looks or character probably see themselves and/or their partner wrongly. The equality of each of us before God needs to be absorbed and differences pooled.

2. Problem-solving is a problem. Some panic. Some blame and don't uncover all that is involved in the issue. Others sublimate problems and pretend they do not exist, when they do. (A problem for one partner is a problem for both.) Others allow it to get out of focus. Others organise furiously, when the issue can be seen another way. Others internalise it and don't share. All problems should occur *within* a relationship of faithfulness and love, and not dominate the marriage.

*3. Reactive relationships are destructive. All of us do many things which are wrong and hurtful. If our partners react in tit for tat terms, then things get progressively worse. The causal chains of evil wrap round a relationship. If, as Jesus tells us to, we return good for evil, then the situation gets progressively better. That requires that our relationship with God is strong and formative.

4. A couple may not share differences, but open them up out of pride. Differences of family background, emotions and personality can become more or less important.

5. One partner conforming to the other or submerging their character in the other is disastrous. Sooner or later one will react, or the other realise that (s)he is married to her/himself. The dynamic of two being in union should continually be present.

6. Withdrawal of love, withdrawal of self and hardening of heart are a crucial and debilitating move. First, the loss of the partner is debilitating, especially the loss of their heart, commitment and sharing. Second, withdrawal of love generates fear, as trust and confidence break down. It is a barrier that there is no way through, and Jesus singled it out for especial attention in relation to divorce. Never have a heart of stone.

7. Anger, irritation and violence are always serious and destructive. They say, I and my will are most important. Get out of my way. Drink, tiredness and stress combine to this pattern and they must be eliminated.

8. Often people escape from relationships which have unsolved problems into television watching, games, hobbies, and various obsessions which obliterate the problem for a while. Escape is a palliative which means that it is not addressed.

9. The fear of divorce and separation can often be built up between a couple by the culture, attitudes of friends and secrecy. Each should *be worthy of* and *give* complete trust.

10. Couples can become isolated from friends, family and

other people through moving, work pressures, commuting, TV and consumption. Because each has to be everything to the other, the internal pressure on this one relationship can be very high. Church, friendship, letterwriting and other networks can overcome this.

11. Hurt caused by abuse, anger, uncaring sex, selfishness, violence and unlove stays with people. Sometimes people hurt back, withdraw or continue to suffer. Hurt needs to be brought to God and sorted out with the spouse.

Work and money

1. Overwork means that marital life is largely marked by fatigue, and the physical inability to give, enjoy and share. A proper discipline of rest is important, as is the ability to resist employers who abuse marriage and family life.

2. Debt is debilitating because it reaches into the future. Irresponsibility in handling money, and hiding it from the partner, are serious breaks of trust. Poverty is better than debt, and debt needs to be faced with help.

3. Economic and financial problems often seem intractable, but usually there is another way of seeing and coping with them. They must be faced together, without unreal blame or self-guilt, and with the willingness to value the marriage and the partner far higher than money. Marriage is for richer, for poorer.

4. Sometimes out of fear couples move towards financial independence and the segregation of work. The fear and these moves should be addressed and reversed.

5. Paid work can be valued more highly than unpaid work. Jobs may have public status which reflects back into the marriage. One may serve the other, who earns the income. Workloads may be unfair. Within the

marriage there should be a deep sense of the mutuality of work, even if one person has to do it all.

6. Consumerism – the belief that buying things offers its own reward, shopping, coveting – wanting goods which are seen as necessary and overcommitment to consumption destroy many relationships. They take up time, demand service and promote debt. Why wash the car when you could wash the wife?

Divorce

Many marriages do end in divorce. An interesting question is whether they should have ended. It is difficult to know accurately, because people will not easily admit that their decision to have a divorce was a mistake. A substantial proportion do recognise this, and more might think in these terms. If we ask what divorce means, there could be a variety of answers. One view is that a spouse leaves his/her partner for someone who is a better person, whatever that means. On this view it is the failure of one partner to come up to the hopes and vision of the other which leads to divorce. Although this might be the view of some divorcees (usually involving a considerable degree of vanity), I doubt that these are the main dynamics. For one thing it needs a pool of better people out there waiting to be snapped up by those who made their first choice, and it is clear the second choice people are not on average going to be better than the first choice people. Rather, divorce is mainly the failure of the marriage relationship. A partner walks out on a relationship in which they have failed and seeks to start again with 'a clean sheet', a vain hope. Often there is culpability. Adultery, violence and unreasonable behaviour do break up marriages, and they should never happen. But at the same time there are marriages which come through even adultery and violence to be good healthy marriages. There are men and women who discover anew how wonderful their partner really is. The clean sheets can occur in the first marriage, if someone does the washing and ironing.

For there is also an inconsistency in the behaviour. Divorcees remarry. Even the trend to cohabitation tends towards permanent relationships. The insistent norm seems to be towards permanent relationships, and the problem is not a failure in the selection process, but a pathology in the character of the marriage relationship. Exactly the same problems which occurred in the first marriage must be worked out in the second. Remarriage is more complex, but not different in character from marriage.

The recovery and enriching of marriages

A marriage is never too far gone to recover, if both partners can be (not are) committed to loving one another. But a person who is emotionally battered may not be able to love for some time. Each person should have a sense that they will be valued and loved and in turn have a commitment to love and respect the other. Christianity does not give up on love. It always hopes and perseveres. Reconstituting the framework of love and trust can be done despite feeling, failure, defeat and even hatred. Love is strong; it keeps no record of wrongs, and can bulldoze on through rough territory being *for* the other person.

Changing from the mentality which walks out on a marriage and looks for a substitute relationship does require a new mindset. It requires partners to consider the extent to which they might be wrong, thoughtless, selfish and cruel. It requires them to seek levels of self-understanding which they have refused earlier. It bids them see their spouse in a way they may have ignored for ten or twenty years. Thus, one of the earliest requirements is for humility and honesty, to undergo the kind of change which is built into the Christian meaning of repentance. Some choose not to go this way. But if the framework of love and faithfulness is shared by a couple, if their lives are open to God and can experience grace and renewal, the marriages can recover. Problems can be sorted out in their proper context, and the richness which is there in each one of us can begin again to be revealed and shared.

17

MARRIAGE RENEWED

The cultural war

We have charted some of the changes which have occurred in marriage in Britain and other parts of the West, especially over the last few decades. The picture is mixed, for it is easy to ignore the fact that a majority of marriages remain intact and are a good part of most people's lives. But the evidence of the level of crisis is also substantial. When 1, 3, 4, or even 5 in 10 marriages break down, the underlying intimate fabric of a society is seriously threatened. Nor is this just a concern for family stability or some kind of social order, for it implies that many people are being seriously hurt and damaged. What some have regarded as an inevitable process or as a pattern of progress cannot be regarded so any longer. The grief which is sometimes publicly expressed, or which we know of through some contact with fragmenting marriages, is but the tip of an iceberg of coldness which has seized many people's lives. This is a major tragedy and crisis. Its impact on people is no less, although less noticeable than a world war. The scale of bereavement and anger which it represents is vast.

Nor can it be interpreted any more in terms of some of the easy answers which have served to sanitise the process. One idea was that couples were incompatible, because they had married the wrong person. The very idea is individualistic and quirky. If there is a certain Mr Right, how it is that he so often turns out to be the boy next door, the bloke at the office or the student down the corridor? 'Whom' a person marries pales into insignificance besides the long-term quality of the relationship. Neither can the idea of the breakdown of a marriage act as a sufficient explanation. A car may break down on a motorway, and it has to be towed away, but if a couple of thousand vehicles give up on the M1, you ask a different kind of question. Clearly, we are not just looking at a number of accidents. The answer has to be cultural, to do with our fundamental attitudes and beliefs. As we have seen, with small families, no war and relative affluence, there is no strong external pressure on marriage. Further, it is quite clear roughly what the culture which has shaped modern marriage is, because it is disseminated on such a large scale. We are bathed in it. It is individualistic humanism, especially as conveyed by a lot of money-making interests which have enormous media and consumption power. But those who push it are winning. They are meeting little cultural resistance, even though what they are selling is often cheap, a lie and feeds on illusion. They have the systems of control in place, and consumers eventually give in. They go for higher salaries, a faster car and glossy sex, but they neglect one another. And there is a deep pride in the process. This is life without God, lived on my terms.

The pace of the cultural change is frightening. We do not yet have a full television generation. Older people still have had a television-free childhood. Yet television exposure is changing us beyond our control. We are soaked in it when young, and most of us will watch at least ten solid years of television during our lives, twenty-four hours a day for 365 days. No longer does family primarily shape marriage for many people, but television does. We are hanging the overwhelming weight of our culture on the screen and much of it is pitiful, mind-numbing stuff. It, and the consumer individualism it peddles, are reshaping marriage. The crisis we are examining is only half-born. In the second half of the crisis a majority of the United States and British populations will not be able to read a book. It is cultural indoctrination, but without a focus. There is no conspiracy, except the search for big money by big corporations. Its dynamics are also out of control. Children of broken marriages are now themselves coming to adulthood on a vast scale. They need time to respond to their past, yet they are being catapulted into their own relationships, under pressure to form them earlier and earlier. Of course, people cope. But we do not know the hardness, indifference and cynicism which are being built into people's intimate lives. Relating which used to be automatic, will become a labour. We are looking at the generation *after* Updike's *Rabbit*.

Christianity and marriage

The response of Christianity has been different from one place to another. In the United States there has been a stronger Christian cultural presence through churches, schools and media, but this sits alongside a major cultural capitulation to individualism. There are many Christians who have accepted many of the trends we have been examining – the search for happiness, work-driven consumerism, egocentric sexual gratification and divorce. The Christian faith has shaped the lives and marriages of many, but many others have been more shaped by the culture of the day. As in the parable of the sower, when the sun came out they withered. The roots were not there. There have been Christian responses, but sometimes they have been limited. They have been *pro-family moralism*, or focused on Christian behaviour, rather than taking in the full scope of what recognising marriage as part of God's creation involved. It is interesting that the Moral Majority has waxed so ireful on abortion, but so dumb on divorce. Why? Probably, because many of its members are compromised on the latter issue. So we find that just 'being Christians' does not make Christian marriages, for the depth of the faith and self-understanding which is required is great. We need to be changed and transformed in ways which are still beyond our conception. There needs to be a deep cultural reformation in relation to God if these intimate relationships are to be transformed.

In Catholic-influenced parts of Europe there has been a better confrontation with the individualist culture. It has been resisted, partly through law, church and the limited impact of television. But the Western individualist culture is wearing away at this resistance, labelling the attitude of upholding marriage and opposing divorce as reactionary, because, of course, more divorce is progress.

But in Britain another pattern obtains. Christians are in a minority of, say, 10 per cent, with a penumbra of 20–30 per cent who are significantly influenced by the Christian faith. Because of the exclusion of the Christian faith from the media and education, the overwhelming majority of younger people have not heard or considered Christianity. In the second half of the twentieth century the Churches have scarcely engaged with the sociological issues of the day, and there has been more focus on weddings than marriages. There is a substantial amount of moralism, but among the younger generation it has been undermined by an individualist reinterpretation, which has rendered much of it contentless. Romantic versions of love and marriage have soured, and although they continue to be presented to each new adolescent cohort, largely the culture is post-romantic. Secular individualism has run riot for decades in popular culture and consumerism, and now it has introjected on many people's ways of thinking, feeling and relating. It is not surprising that Britain is one of the leading countries for divorce.

None of this has been confronted culturally by the Churches in any significant way. Indeed, the normal stance of liberal theologians has been to run after a movement in this culture, usually ten years late, without seeing the underlying cultural difference between Christianity and this modern secularism. In the 1960s some theologians ran after existentialism, in the 1970s phenomenology, in the 1980s interpretive theology and in the 1990s postmodernism. What is sad is that they have often failed to see the internal critique which was developed in each of these patterns of thought and culture. To a considerable extent postmodernism is calling into question a range of the modern meta-narratives like progress, rational thought, science, technology, individual freedom and knowledge as incontrovertible. It has pulled away the tables on which this liberal theology was based. In sexual and marital areas there was a similar record. *Marriage, Divorce and the Church* (Church of England, 1971) assumed that the dominance of liberal culture was inevitable. The Report, *Something to Celebrate*, although it had some valuable recommendations in social policy and pastoral support, was basically seeking to affirm whatever subjective views of marriage and the family might happen to exist (Church of England, 1995, 66). Its starting-point was a deconstructionist view of the family (Barton, 1993) and, although it moved on from that position, it never had a viewpoint which broke free from the affirmation of subjectively generated lifestyles.

The reaction to it summarised where our culture has been in the 1990s. Some moralists saw a stupid, but innocuous, remark about 'living in sin' as the moral bandwagon on which they wanted to climb in order to attack the Report. Progressive individualists saw it as the Church of England trying again to become more contentless in faith and up to date, and patronised it. But the dominant reaction by far seemed to be of those who had experienced the liberal and individualist culture in sex and marriage for several decades, but knew there was not so much to celebrate. Broken marriages and families were and are problems which need facing and reflecting on soberly, because so many have been hurt. Many of the more reflective people were angry that this report had side-stepped this issue. If you've just had a driving accident, you don't have a party, but find out what the damage is and reassess your driving. There has been a growing sense that the time for assessment has come, and this document had failed to do it.

Why it failed is worth some reflection. One explanation was a long-term weakness in social theology and biblical study. Another was the uncritical internal links between liberal culture and theology. But another cause was more immediate. My perception was that one of the chief stumbling blocks was the relationship of moralism to the Church. It is easy to see some members of the churches as traditionalists, who want to 'return to traditional morality'. Along with this package goes, it is assumed, judgementalism and rule-bound activity. Over against this, the escape from moralism and judgementalism is an espousal of where people are and an affirmation of them as people. These alternatives are both, of course, misconceived and disastrous. The New Testament contains the most devastating critique of moralism and judgementalism. The point is never what we think of others or others of us, because all social judgements are made, as Jesus pointed out, by those with a log in their own eye. The moralists are those who have transferred the focus from God to themselves. James makes the point in his letter: 'Brothers and sisters, do not slander one another. Anyone who speaks against another or judges them, speaks against the law and judges it. When you judge the law, you are not keeping it, but sitting in judgement on it. There is only one Lawgiver and Judge' (Jas. 4:11–12). The answer to moralism is always to refocus on God, and regain some humility, not to give up on morality and right living. In its desire to avoid moralism, the Report sometimes lost the Christian focus on God's right ways for us as a universal blessing. We do not have to be either moralist, or antimoralist, but just Christian.

The Christian scenario is thus not very good. In the United States, although there is some good Christian marital and family life, it is less noisy than many other patterns which are hypocritical and deeply influenced by modern individualism and more publicity. In more Catholic countries Christian principles are often portrayed as reactionary and face tremendous commercial pressure. In Britain Christian reactions have been confused and confusing, and the wider public has scarcely heard anything that amounts to a coherent Christian witness in marriage and family life, although again there are many good Christian marriages which speak beyond words. Often the message which comes across is just a commitment to family services in church. We should be able to do better than this, but it requires that we recognise the depth of the problem. Problems in marriage centrally engage with our relationship with God, with the meaning of life and how we live. The issue will not be solved through publicity, publications or how-to manuals, but by addressing these great issues that we face in our lives through and in the terms of the Christian faith.

The Crisis Addressed

This Christian scenario is, however, lagging behind wider Western societies. Here, we have to face the fact that we do not know sociologically what is happening. The changes are occurring too fast for us to understand. We cannot evaluate the impact of television on married life; a full TV generation has not yet gone through, and the scale and content of television is constantly changing. We do not yet know fully the impact of marital breakdown on children, the effects of working mothers, of earlier and wider sexual experience, of pornography, of rich homes, of overwork. This lack of sociological perspective mirrors what is happening in the lives of many couples. They do, after all, get married in vast numbers. Overwhelmingly, they believe in marriage or even in cohabitation. Yet so many of these relationships do not 'work out'. This suggests that people are not in control. It is an odd failure. In a culture where we put the greatest premium on being in control of events and life, 'it seems to be running us. Before a couple can respond to a growing problem, they are precipitated on to divorce. Thus, personally, many of us are struggling with relational problems which are too big for us. We are tumbling in the big wave or are at least pulled by strong currents. Being hurt, defeated, living with what should never have been, escaping bitterness and regaining some self-esteem are often ignored in the wider culture, but it is what many of us spend our time doing.

It is a crisis which is spreading by age. The old are dying and the young are born and come to maturity. The older generation had often faced war and poverty, but they had firm marriages and worked together for their kids. The young have television, film, sex and often problematic relationships. The old are dying, and we are quietly losing many good marriages. They tend to be replaced by broken relationships, cohabitation and fractured child-care. It is also spreading world-wide. Westernism is transforming cultures around the world. It is spreading in from the coasts of Africa and South America; it is mimicked in Eastern Asia. Although India cannot easily be materialistic, because it is so poor, it can appropriate Western romanticism to its own epic literature and school hundreds of millions of Indian girls to yearn for romantic love. Above all, it is spreading by media culture. Millions learn through the media, but they do not learn as Western intellectuals, in control, evaluating and weighing, but as animals led by the nose. Media people are very clever, but for many their cleverness extends only to the manipulation and deception of their audiences. They aim to capture them, to make them addicts, and they will tell them whatever lies are necessary so to do. The result has been a vast culture of deception in relation to marriage, intimacy, sex and family life which is now so normal that it is not questioned. Of course a family sitcom will give a cosy laugh a minute and make sure that no one is really hurt; if audiences want a sedative, we will lay it on. Of course pin-ups smile: you wouldn't want to see them grumpy would you? The power of this deception, in my opinion, makes Rupert Murdoch and the other media barons among those who are more responsible for evil, whether they know it or not, than any others of this generation. The motive is financial gain, and its outcome is levels of personal deception and breakdown which we cannot comprehend.

But the crisis is also intimate and personal. It is made up of parents worrying about the relationships and culture of their children, not because they do not love or trust them, but because the evidence is around of false answers which children can easily espouse. Children are taught that all relationships are bargaining: life is being good for a packet of sweets. A young woman expects she will not find a man she can trust. A man knows he will be ignored, because he has no chance of obtaining a good job. A father knows that two-week visits to his children are unnatural, will not really work and drops out into parental anonymity. These situations are common and do not come from outside. The media is part of the picture, but these are our lives. We craft the outcome of our own relationships. They reflect our personal culture, our faith, our commitments and our values. The insistent conclusion, therefore, is that our *faith* is the great social variable in this crisis.

We may say that individualism and self-referential lives are the way to live, that we can accommodate to the crisis and manage our relationships on our own terms. But this book disagrees. Our culture has been feeding in a far country, it has been eating food without nourishment and is in crisis. And the crisis cannot be addressed in terms of individualism, materialism or even some conservative set of family values. The answer is not to be found in books on 'how to improve your sex life' or other techniques of relationship manipulation. It involves at the deepest level whether we are going to live in intimate relationship in God's way or our own. This question is already being answered in one way or the other by millions of marriages, and the failure of a self-made culture point to the change of faith which is required.

This change in faith and culture is massive, but also quite intimate. It can happen in the lives of individuals and couples, and it can also be reflected in the media, economics and law. The Christian understanding of marriage and family does not come to any of us as outsiders, but addresses us as who we are, and the root changes are therefore deeper than just social or economic, although they are that as well. They are Christian truths to be recovered, or known for the first time by an individualistic culture, which interpret us and the meaning of our relationships. Our personal identity is to be found in our relationship with the Creator. We are created to live in obedience to norms which are the condition for good relationships. Marriage *is* a created structure for our good. Love works, even though it is costly. Identifying sin before it traps and defeats us is important. Men and women are *for* one another. The right way to live is often deeper than our own shallow understanding; we walk by faith not by sight. We cannot serve God and Mammon. Lust and adultery are wrong. This is understanding which pushes us beyond ourselves and our own relationships into acknowledging again the centrality of God in human existence and relationships. We are defined by the law and precepts of our Creator. There is a necessary human dependence on Jesus's teaching; it gives us insights into ourselves and a knowledge of God which come no other way. Jesus's death and resurrection address the deepest failures of our lives. There *is* Good News for all marriages. The aim of this book is to convey again some of Christian truth and insight which has shaped and transformed the lives and marriages of millions. It addresses us as we are. It is God with us. It is the abiding and trustworthy love of Jesus Christ, and it makes 'for better, for worse' always for better.

Bibliography

Chapter 1   Western marriage

Lerone Bennett, *Before the Mayflower* (Penguin, 1966).

Christopher Brook, *The Medieval Idea of Marriage* (Oxford University Press, 1989).

Jacob Burckhardt, *The Civilisation of the Renaissance in Italy* (Phaidon, 1965).

Simone De Beauvoir, *The Second Sex* (Penguin, 1972).

Denis De Rougemont, *Love in the Western World* (Princeton University Press, 1983).

Ronald Fletcher, *The Family and Marriage in Britain* (Penguin, 1966).

John Gillis, *For Better for Worse: British Marriages, 1600 to the Present* (Oxford University Press, 1985).

John Goldthorpe, *Family Life in Western Societies* (Cambridge University Press, 1987).

Ronald Frankenberg, *Communities in Britain* (Penguin, 1966).

Gertrude Himmelfarb, *The Demoralisation of Society* (IEA, 1995).

David Hunter, *Marriage in the Early Church* (Fortress Press, 1992).

Winthrop Jordan, *White over Black* (Penguin, 1969).

Stephen Ozment, *When Fathers Ruled: Family Life in Reformation Europe* (Harvard University Press, 1983).

Ronald Pearsall, *The Worm in the Bud* (Penguin, 1971).

Sarah Pomeroy, *Goddesses, Whores, Wives and Slaves: Women in Classical Antiquity* (Schocken, 1975).

Mario Praz, *The Romantic Agony* (Oxford University Press, 1970).

Stuart Queen, *et al.*, *The Family in Various Cultures*, 5th edn (Harper and Row, 1985).

Edward Shorter, *The Making of the Modern Family* (Basic, 1975).

Lawrence Stone, *The Family, Sex and Marriage in England 1500–1800* (Harper and Row, 1977).

Alan Storkey, *The Epistemological Foundations of Consumption Theory* (Vrije Universiteit Press, 1993).

Alan Storkey, *The Meanings of Love* (IVP, 1994).

Susan Treggiari, *Roman Marriage: Iusti Coniuges from the Time of Cicero to the Time of Ulpian* (Oxford University Press, 1993).

Thorsten Veblen, *The Place of Science in Modern Civilisation and Other Essays* (Caprice, 1969 [1915]).

Arthur Waley, *Chinese Poems* (Unwin, 1960).

Ernest Westermarck, *The History of Human Marriage*, 3 vols, 5th edn (Macmillan, 1925 [1891]).

Michael Young and Peter Willmott, *Family and Kinship in East London* (Penguin, 1962).

Chapter 2   Marriage in crisis?

Church of England Board of Social Responsibility, *Something to Celebrate* (Church House, 1995).

David Cooper, *The Death of the Family* (Penguin, 1972).

Ronald Fletcher, *The Abolitionists* (Routledge, 1988).

Michel Foucault, *The History of Sexuality*, 2 vols (Penguin, 1981, 1987).

Julian Hafner, *The End of Marriage* (Century, 1993).

Helen Kaplan, *The New Sex Therapy* (Times Books, 1974).

R. D. Laing and A. Esterton, *Sanity, Madness and the Family* (Pelican, 1970).

Edmund Leach, *The Listener*, 30 November 1967, p. 695.

William Masters, Virginia Johnson and Robert Kolodny, *Human Sexuality* (HarperCollins, 1992).

Thomas McGinnis and Dana Finnegan, *Open Family and Marriage* (Mosby, 1976).

Glenda Riley, *Divorce: An American Tradition* (Oxford University Press, 1991).

Social Trends (HMSO, 1995).

Alan Storkey, *The Meanings of Love* (IVP, 1994).

Kaye Wellings *et al.*, *Sexual Behaviour in Britain* (Penguin, 1995).

Chapter 3   A Christian understanding of marriage

Dan Allender and Tremper Longman, *Bold Love* (Navpress, 1992).

David Atkinson, *To Have and To Hold* (Collins, 1979).

Jack and Judith Balswick, *The Family: A Christian Perspective* (Baker Book House, 1991).

Michael and Myrtle Baughen, *Your Marriage* (Hodder and Stoughton, 1994).

Christopher Brooke, *The Medieval Idea of Marriage* (Oxford University Press, 1989).

Emil Brunner, *Love and Marriage: Selections from the Divine Imperative* (Fontana, 1970).

John Calvin, *Institutes of the Christian Religion* (James Clarke, 1962).

Andrew Cornes, *Divorce and Remarriage* (Hodder and Stoughton, 1993).

Abdur Rahman I Doi, *Shari'ah: The Islamic Law* (Ta Ha, 1984).

Jack Dominion, *Marriage, Faith and Love* (Darton, Longman and Todd, 1981).

Jack Dominion, *Marriage: The Definitive Guide to What Makes a Marriage Work* (Heinemann, 1995).

Herman Dooyeweerd, *A New Critique of Theoretical Thought* (Pres. and Reformed, 1954) vol. III, 305–41.

David Hunter, *Marriage in the Early Church* (Fortress Press, 1992).

Sören Kierkegaard, *The Works of Love* (Harper, 1962).

Ferdinand Mount, *The Subversive Family* (Unwin, 1983).

James Olthius, *I Pledge You my Troth* (Harper and Row, 1976).

Otto Piper, *The Biblical View of Sex and Marriage* (James Nisbet, 1960).

Stuart Queen *et al.*, *The Family in Various Cultures*, 5th edn (Harper and Row, 1985).

Edward Schillebeeckx, *Marriage: Human Reality and Saving Mystery* (Sheed and Ward, 1965).

Alan Storkey, *A Christian Social Perspective* (IVP, 1979).

Elaine Storkey, *What's Right with Feminism?* (SPCK, 1985).

Susan Treggiari, *Roman Marriage* (Clarendon Press, 1991).

Chapter 4　Marriages and the families of origin

John Bowlby, *Child Care and the Growth of Love* (Penguin, 1953).

Moncrieff Cochran *et al.*, *Extending Families* (Cambridge University Press, 1990).

Pamela Cotterill, *Friendly Relations? Mothers and their Daughters in Law* (Taylor and Francis, 1994).

Erik Erikson, *Childhood and Society* (Paladin, 1977 [1951]).

Janet Finch, *Family Obligations and Social Change* (Polity Press, 1989).

Nancy Friday, *My Mother My Self* (Fontana, 1977).

Shere Hite, *The Hite Report on the Family* (Bloomsbury, 1995).

Richard Hoggart, *The Uses of Literacy* (Penguin, 1958); and *A Local Habitation: Vol. 1, Life and Times 1918–40* (Chatto and Windus, 1988).

Steve Humphries and Pamela Gordon, *A Labour of Love: The Experience of Parenthood in Britain 1900–1950* (Sidgewick and Jackson, 1993).

R. D. Laing and Aaron Esterton, *Sanity, Madness and the Family* (Pelican, 1970).

John and Elizabeth Newson, *Seven Years Old in the Home Environment* (Penguin, 1978).

Peter Reider and Clare Lucey (eds), *Assessment of Parenting* (Routledge, 1995).
Corrie Ten Boom, *The Hiding Place* (Hodder and Stoughton, 1971).
Mark Twain, *The Adventures of Tom Sawyer*.
C. W. Valentine, *The Normal Child and Some of his Abnormalities* (Penguin, 1956).

Chapter 5   Friends, dating and mating

Karl Barth, *Church Dogmatics* (T & T Clark, 1958).
Emil Brunner, *Love and Marriage* (Fontana, 1970 [1937]).
William Bukowski (ed.), *The Company They Keep: Friendships in Childhood and Adolescence* (Cambridge University Press, 1996).
Peter Chambers, *Made in Heaven?* (SPCK, 1988).
Kaye Cook and Lance Lee, *Man and Woman, Alone and Together* (Bridge Point, 1992).
Rodney Court and Sally Lloyd, *Courtship* (Sage, 1992).
Michel Foucault, *The History of Sexuality* 2 vols (Penguin, 1981, 1987).
William Masters *et al.*, *Human Sexuality* (HarperCollins, 1992).
Josh McDowell, *Why Wait?* (HLP, 1987).
Michael Schofield, *The Sexual Behaviour of Young People* (Pelican, 1969).
Kaye Wellings *et al.*, *Sexual Behaviour in Britain* (Penguin, 1995).
Veronica Zundel, *Going Out* (Hodder and Stoughton, 1990).

Chapter 6   Cohabitation

Chris Barton, *Cohabitation Contracts* (Gower, 1985).
Bram Buunk and Barry Van Driel, *Variant Lifestyles and Relationships* (Sage, 1989).

Jeremy Collingwood, *Common Law Marriage: The Case for a Change in the Law* (Grove, 1994).

Duncan Dormor, *The Relationship Revolution: Cohabitation, Marriage and Divorce in Contemporary Europe* (One plus One, 1992).

Greg Forster, *Cohabitation and Marriage* (Marshall Pickering, 1994).

David Hall and John Rhao, 'Cohabitation and Divorce in Canada: Testing the Selectivity Hypothesis', *Journal of Marriage and Family*, 57, May 1995, 421–7.

J. Haskey, 'Premarital cohabitation and the probabilities of subsequent divorce', *Population Trends*, 68, 1992.

Gary Jenkins, *Cohabitation: A Biblical Perspective* (Grove, 1992).

Kathleen Kiernan and Valerie Estaugh, *The Rise of Cohabitation and Childbearing outside Marriage* (Rowntree Foundation, 1993).

Wendy Manning, 'Cohabitation, Marriage, and Entry into Motherhood', *JMF*, 1995, 191–200.

Susan McRae, *Cohabiting Mothers* (Policy Studies Institute, 1993).

Social Trends (HMSO, 1995).

Jan Stets, 'Cohabiting and Marital Agression: The Role of Social Isolation', *JMF*, 53, Aug. 1991, 669–80.

Kaye Wellings, *Sexual Behaviour in Britain* (Penguin, 1995).

Geertje Wiersma, *Cohabitation, an Alternative to Marriage? A Cross-national Study* (Martinus Nijhoff, 1983).

Stephen S. Williams, 'I will: the debate about cohabitation', *Anvil*, vol. 10, no. 3, 1993, 209–24.

Chapter 7   Faith and marriage

Zakaria Bashier, *Muslim Women in the Midst of Change* (Islamic Foundation, 1985).

Jeanne Becher (ed.), *Women, Religion and Sexuality* (WCC, 1991).

Christopher Buule, *The Ring and the Rib* (Oak Hill, 1985).

Abdur Rahman I Doi, *Shari'ah: The Islamic Law* (Ta Ha, 1984).

Joy Hendry, *Marriage in Changing Japan* (Croom Helm, 1981).

Fatima Mernissi, *Women and Islam* (Blackwell, 1991).

David Parkin and David Nyamwaya, *Transformations of African Marriage* (Manchester University Press, 1987).

Diana Paul, *Women in Buddhism* (University of California Press, 1985).

Ursula Sharma, *Women's Work, Class and the Urban Household: A Study of Shimla, North India* (Tavistock, 1986).

Chapter 8   Sex and marriage

Phillipe Ariès and André Bégin, *Western Sexuality* (Basil Blackwell, 1985).

Anthony Copley, *Sexual Moralities in France 1780–1980* (Routledge, 1989).

Helen Crowley and Susan Himmelweit (eds), *Knowing Women* (Polity Press/Open University, 1992).

Rita Freedman, *Beauty Bound* (Columbus, 1988).

Peter Gardella, *Innocent Ecstasy* (Oxford University Press, 1985).

Anthony Giddens, *The Transformation of Intimacy* (Polity Press, 1992).

J. Holland *et al.* 'Pressured Pleasure: Young Women and the Negotiation of Sexual Boundaries', *Sociological Review*, Nov. 1992, 647–73.

Annette Lawson, *Adultery: An Analysis of Love and Betrayal* (Oxford University Press, 1988).

William Masters, Virginia Johnson and Robert Kolodny, *Human Sexuality*, (HarperCollins, 1992).

Anders Nygren, *Agape and Eros* (SPCK, 1932).

Otto Piper, *The Biblical View of Sex and Marriage* (Nisbet, 1960).

Edward Shorter, *A History of Women's Bodies* (Basic Books, 1982).

Gerda Siann, *Gender, Sex and Sexuality* (Taylor and Francis, 1994).

Jeffrey Weeks, *Sex, Politics and Society* (Longmans, 1981).

Chapter 9   Marriage and people

G. C. Berkouwer, *Man: The Image of God* (Eerdmans, 1962).

Anne Borrowdale, *A Woman's Work* (SPCK, 1989).

Arnold De Graaf *et al.*, *Towards a Biblical View of Man* (Institute of Christian Studies, 1978).

Dick Keyes, *Beyond Identity* (Hodder and Stoughton, 1984).

Gordon Spykman, *Reformational Theology* (Eerdmans, 1992), 195–267.

Alan Storkey, *A Christian Social Perspective* (IVP, 1979).

Charles Taylor, *Sources of the Self* (Cambridge University Press, 1989).

Paul Tournier, *The Strong and the Weak* (SCM, 1963).

Chapter 10   Gender and marriage

Jesse Bernard, *The Female World* (Free Press, 1981).

Christopher Clulow (ed.), *Women, Men and Marriage* (SPCK/Tavistock, 1995).

Gretchen Gaebelein Hull, *Equal to Serve* (Scripture Union, 1987).

Eva Gamarnikow *et al.* (eds), *The Public and the Private* (Heinemann, 1983).

Christine Gerachty, *Women and Soap Opera* (Polity Press, 1991).

John Gray, *Men are from Mars, Women are from Venus* (HarperCollins, 1992).

Suzette Hadenelgin, *Genderspeak: Men, Women and the Gentle Art of Verbal Self-defense* (Wiley, 1993).

Joke Hermson and Alkeline Van Lemming (eds), *Sharing the Difference* (Routledge, 1991).

Blanche Hersh, *The Slavery of Sex: Feminist Abolitionists in America* (University of Illinois Press, 1978).

Michael Kimmel and Michael Messner (eds), *Men's Lives* (Macmillan, 1989).

Aaron Kipnis and Elizabeth Herron, *Gender War, Gender Peace* (William Morrow, 1994).

Roy McCloughry, *Men and Masculinity* (Hodder and Stoughton, 1992).

Lynne Segal, *Slow Motion: Changing Masculinities, Changing Men* (Virago, 1990).

Dale Spender, *Man-Made Language* (Routledge, Kegan and Paul, 1985).

Elaine Storkey, *What's Right with Feminism* (SPCK, 1985).

Elaine Storkey, *The Search for Intimacy* (Hodder and Stoughton, 1995).

Deborah Tannen, *You Just Don't Understand: Women and Men in Conversation* (William Morrow, 1990).

Deborah Tannen, *Talking from 9 to 5* (William Morrow, 1994).
Carol Tavris, *The Mismeasure of Women* (Simon and Schuster, 1992).

Mary Stewart Van Leeuwen, *Gender and Grace* (Inter-Varsity Press, 1990).

Sylvia Walby, *Patriarchy at Work* (Polity Press, 1986).

Yvette Walczak, *He and She: Men in the Eighties* (Routledge, 1988).

Chapter 11   The emotions of marriage

Dan Allender, *The Wounded Heart: Hope for Adult Victims of Child Sexual Abuse* (NavPress, 1990).

Dan Allender, *Bold Love* (NavPress, 1992).

Eliana Gil, *Treatment of Adult Survivors of Childhood Abuse* (Launch Press, 1988).

Tony Gough, *Couples Arguing* (Darton, Longman and Todd, 1987).

Archibald Hart, *Me, Myself and I* (Highland, 1992).

Anne Long, *Listening* (DLT, 1990).

Alan Storkey, *The Meanings of Love* (IVP, 1994).
Paul Tournier, *Escape from Loneliness* (SCM, 1962).
Paul Tournier, *Creative Suffering* (SCM, 1982).

Chapter 12   Marriage and work

Sheila Allen and Carol Wolkowitz, *Homeworking: Myths and Realities* (Macmillan, 1987).
Lambros Comitas and David Lowenthal (eds), *Work and Family Life: West Indian Perspectives* (Anchor, 1973).
Norman Dennis *et al.*, *Coal is our Life* (Tavistock, 1959).
Shirley Dex, *The Sexual Division of Work* (Harvester, 1985).
Marian Edelman, *Families in Peril* (Harvard University Press, 1987).
Stephen Edgell, *Middle Class Couples: A Study of Segregation, Domination and Inequality in Marriage* (George Allen and Unwin, 1980).
Michael Fogarty, Rhona Rapoport and Robert Rapoport, *Sex, Career and Family* (George Allen and Unwin, 1971).
Lucia Gilbert, *Men in Dual-Career Families* (Lawrence Erlbaum Associates, 1985).
John Goldthorpe *et al.*, *The Affluent Worker in the Class Structure* (Cambridge University Press, 1969).
Bob Holman, *Putting Families First* (Macmillan, 1988).
Mirra Komarovsky, *Blue-Collar Marriage* (Yale University Press, 1962).
Nicola Madge (ed.), *Families at Risk* (Heinemann, 1983).
Peter Moss and Nickie Fonda (eds), *Work and the Family* (Temple Smith, 1980).
Alva Myrdal and Viola Klein, *Women's Two Roles* (Routledge and Kegan Paul, 1956).
Rob Parsons, *The Sixty Minute Father* (Hodder and Stoughton, 1995).
Wade and Mary Rowatt, *The Two-Career Marriage* (Westminster, 1980).
Joan Smith and Immanuel Wallerstein, *Creating and Transforming Households* (Cambridge University Press, 1992).

Social Trends (HMSO, 1994, 1995).
Alan Storkey, *Transforming Economics* (SPCK, 1986) ch 9.

Chapter 13   Marriage and home life

Michael Anderson *et al.* (eds), *The Social and Political Economy of the Household* (Oxford University Press, 1994).
Anne Borrowdale, *A Woman's Work* (SPCK, 1989).
David Clark, (ed.), *Marriage, Domestic Life and Social Change: Writings for Jacqueline Burgoyne* (Routledge, 1991).
Eva Garmarnikow *et al.* (eds), *The Public and the Private* (Heinemann, 1983).
Naomi Gerstel and Harriet Gross, *Commuter Marriage* (The Guilford Press, 1984).
Ann Oakley, *Housewife* (Penguin, 1976).
Rob Shields (ed.), *Lifestyle Shopping* (Routledge, 1992).
Alan Storkey, *Epistemological Foundations of Consumption Theory* (Free University Press, 1993).
John Tiemstra *et al.*, *Reforming Economics* (Edwin Mellon Press, 1990).
Tony Walter, *All you Love is Need* (SPCK, 1985).
Gail Wilson, *Money in the Family* (Avebury, 1987).

Chapter 14   The stages of marriage

David and Vera Mace, *We Can Have Better Marriages* (Marshall, Morgan and Scott, 1975).
Ann Oakley, *From Here to Maternity* (Penguin, 1981).
Jim Olthius, *Keeping our Troth* (Harper and Row, 1986).
K. Warner Schaie and Sherry Willis, *Adult Development and Aging* (HarperCollins, 1991).
Gail Sheehy, *Passages: Predictable Crises of Adult Life* (Bantam, 1976).
James Thompson *et al.*, *Ageing* (BSR/Church House, 1990).

Sara Wenger Shenk, *And Then There Were Three* (Herald, 1985).

Chapter 15   Law and marriage

P. M. Bromley, *Family Law* (Butterworths).
Butterworths *Family Law* (Butterworths).
Church of England, *Putting Asunder: A Divorce Law for Contemporary Society* (SPCK, 1966).
Lord Mackay, *Looking to the Future* (HMSO, Cm 2799, 1995).
D. Tolstoy, *Divorce* (Sweet and Maxwell).
James Wilson *et al.* (eds), *Just a Piece of Paper? Divorce Reform and the Undermining of Marriage* (IEA, 1995).

Chapter 16   Marital breakdown and recovery

Theodor Bovet, *A Handbook to Marriage and Marriage Guidance* (Longmans, Green and Co., 1958).
Melanie Carew-Jones and Hestor Watson, *Making the Break: For Women Experiencing Violence* (Penguin, 1985).
Andrew Cornes, *Divorce and Remarriage* (Hodder and Stoughton, 1993).
Tony Gough, *Couples Growing* (Darton, Longman and Todd, 1992).
Sarah Litvinoff, *The Relate Guide to Better Relationships* (Vermilion, 1992).
David and Vera Mace, *We Can Have Better Marriages* (Marshall, Morgan and Scott, 1974).
Lily Pincus (ed.), *Studies in Emotional Conflict* (Tavistock Centre, 1973).
Paul Tournier, *Marriage Difficulties* (SCM, 1967).

Chapter 17   Marriage renewed

Stephen Barton, 'Towards a Theology of the Family', *Crucible*, Jan/March, 1993.

Francis Bridger, *Celebrating the Family: A Critique* (Grove, 1995).

Church of England Board of Social Responsibility, *Something to Celebrate* (Church House Publishing, 1995).

Commission of Archbishop of Canterbury, *Marriage, Divorce and the Church* (SPCK, 1971).

Alan Storkey, *Marriage, Divorce and the Church: A Review* (Shaftesbury Project, 1971).

John Updike, *Rabbit Redux* (André Deutsch, 1972).

INDEX

abortions, 82
Abraham, 7
accommodating, 137–8
action man, 146–7
adultery, 4, 20, 56, 113–14, 126–7,
    198–202
affinity relationships, 59–60
Africa, 5, 6, 8, 50, 109, 221
ancestor worship, 5, 7
anorexia, 119
arguments, 137, 158–9, 179
arranged marriages, 5–7, 47
Augustine, 133

barriers, 158–9
Barton, C., 97–8
Barton, S., 218
beauty, 130
Black families, 8, 28, 95–7, 171
bodies, 118–20, 125–6
bonding, 158–9
breadwinner, 144, 164–7

Calvin, J., 38–9, 114
career, 164–70, 172–3
Catholic Church, 21, 42, 92, 217–9
chastity, 80–1
children, 59–76, 155–8
China, 1, 5, 6–7, 12, 108
Christianity, 2–5, 7, 10, 14–16,
    35–58, 102–3, 109, 140–1,
    182–4, 216–20
Church, 15, 102, 216–20
Church of England, 10, 194, 197,
    218–19
cohabitation, 28, 92–105
common law marriages, 92
Communist Manifesto, 9
communication, 25, 63–4, 149–51,
    183–90, 205–6
commuter marriages, 164, 168–70

concubines, 6
conflict, 158–9
Confucianism, 7–8
conjugal family, 59–60
consanguineal relations, 59
consumerism, 31, 82, 165, 172–3
contractual marriage, 16–17, 28,
    97–8
control, 8–10, 31–2, 56–8, 130,
    143–4, 148–9
courtship, 47, 84–7, 89–91
convenantal marriage, 40
creation, 3–4, 36–44, 48–9,
    118–20, 131
creativity, 145–6
crime, 177

Daly, Arthur, 146
dating, 84–7
De Beauvoir, S., 12
de-resourced class, 171
definition of cohabitation, 92–3
definition of marriage, 35–6, 58
depression, 68, 189–90
desertion, 158–9
divorce, 4, 20–4, 74–5, 104–5,
    110, 192–202, 211–12
domination, 137–8, 184, 186
double standard, 80–1
dualisms, 134–5

egoism, 16–17, 30, 33, 43, 112,
    131, 161, 184
embourgeoisement, 170–1
emotional hiss, 161
emotions, 153–63
employers, 29, 98–9, 169–70
endogamy, 47, 86
engagement, 86
Engels, F., 9
Enlightenment, 11

Europe, 6, 21–2, 29, 62–3, 96, 101–3, 169, 217
evil, 132–3, 157
egogamy, 47, 86
extended family, 60

faith, 75–6, 106–117, 222–3
faithfulness, 53–5
family biography, 62–4
family-dominated marriage, 5–8, 59–60
family dynasties, 5
family life, 185–6
fathers and marriage, 48, 60–75, 94
father figure, 71
father hunger, 74–5
fatigue, 187
Feminism, 10, 139–41, 150
fixated persons, 131
Fletcher, R., 18
Foucault, M., 81
freedom, 130–2
Freud, S., 15, 81
friendship, 53, 77–91, 178
Functionalism, 39

gender, 49, 71, 139–52, 166–7
Germany, 1, 21, 169
Giddens, A., 121
God, 3, 11, 14, 27–8, 35–46, 53–8, 62, 72, 75–9, 83, 88, 90–1, 97, 102, 106–7, 111–22, 124, 129–34, 138, 146–7, 153–4, 157–8, 160–3, 173, 179, 184–92, 204–11, 213, 215–20, 222–3
Godfather, 5
grandparents, 60–4

Hafner, J., 23
'headship', 57–8
hedonism, 16
helper, 36–7, 56–7
heterogamy, 86
hijab, 110
Hinduism 7, 108–9
Hite, S., 69

Holy Spirit, 35, 113, 118, 130, 132, 138, 144
home, 148, 174–81
holiness, 133–5
Holman, B., 171
Holocaust, 62–3
homogamy, 86
homosexuality, 49
humanism, 11–13, 38
husband control, 56
husband-directed marriage, 44
hypergamy, 85
hypogamy, 85

ideal/real dualism, 37, 134–5, 176–8
identity, 44, 75–6, 129–38
idolatry, 131
incest taboo, 40–1, 69
India, 6–7, 108, 165
individualism, 15–17, 22–4, 26–8, 30, 184, 215–16
institutions, 38–9, 41–3
intimacy, 95, 162–3
Islam, 7, 50, 109–10

Japan, 5, 6–7, 12, 88–9, 108, 169
jealousy, 55–6
Jesus Christ, 4, 16, 35–7, 54, 57–8, 66, 77–9, 87, 114–16, 127, 130, 132–3, 139, 144, 148, 156–7, 172–3, 179, 183, 186, 204–5, 209, 219, 223
Jews, 2, 62, 136
Judas, 78
Judaeo-Christian tradition, 49, 107, 111–12, 192
justice, 194–5

kinship, 59–60
Kuyper, A., 42

law, 15, 84, 192–202
Lawrence, D. H., 82
Laing, R. D., 23, 67
Leach, E., 23
leisure, 26, 142–3, 145–6, 168
liberal culture, 19–20, 33, 81–2, 193–8

Liverpool, 9
London, 7, 29, 120
loneliness, 28
love, 27, 38–9, 53, 160, 206–7, 223

Mackay, Lord, 194–8
Mafia, 7
male initiation, 72
Man worship, 11–13
manipulation, 137
marital abuse, 179
marital breakdown, 203–13, 215
Marriage and
  children, 65–7
  covenant, 40
  crisis of, 20–2, 214–23
  equality in, 56–8
  heterosexual, 48–9
  institution of, 36–40
  Judaeo-Christian, 2–5
  law, 102, 192–202
  persons, 27–8, 129–38
  scapegoating, 23
  stages, 182–91
  union, 3–4, 17, 35, 50–2, 200, 209
  universality of, 1–2, 106–7
  voluntary, 5, 46–7
  wrong reasons for, 79, 89
Marriage and family as two
        institutions, 4, 40–1
Marx, K., 9
mating, 85–91
matriarchal families, 7, 56
matrilineal families, 6, 60
matrilocal marriage, 6, 174
Matrimonial Causes Act, 1973,
        194, 197–8
midlife, 188–90
monogamy, 3, 49–50
Moral Majority, 16, 216
moralism, 14–16, 216–17
Mormons, 50
Mosaic law, 3–4, 192
mother–daughter/wife
        relationship, 70–1, 95–7
mother–son/husband relationship,
        73
mother-in-law problem for
        husband, 71

mother-in-law problem for wife,
        6, 73
Mount, F., 42
moving home, 174–5, 178
Murdoch, R., 221
mutuality, 36–7

neolocal marriage, 174–5, 178
New Wet Male, 95
newly-weds, 183–5
no-fault divorce, 23–4, 193–5
nuclear families, 31, 60, 174–81

Oedipal theory, 73
outdoors/indoors, 110, 146
overwork, 29, 165–70, 172–3, 177,
        186
parental deficit, 74–5
parents and marriage, 59–75
passive father, 96, 166–7
paterfamilias, 6
patriarchs, 3, 5, 7, 49
patriarchy, 10, 56, 71–2
patrilineal family, 6, 60
patrilocal marriage, 6, 174
Paul, Apostle, 16, 45–6, 87, 100,
        102, 107, 118, 122, 125
permissive sexuality, 94
personhood, 43–5, 50, 129–38
plastic sex, 121
play, 142–3
pluralism – horizontal, 41–2,
        vertical, 195–6
polyandry, 50
polygamy, 3, 49–50, 110
polygyny, 49
pornography, 30–1, 84, 123
postmodernism, 217–8
post-romanticism, 27, 94
poverty, 28–9
power, 8–10, 31–2, 56–8
prayer, 55
premarital cohabitation, 99–101
premarital sex, 14, 26, 47, 80–4
privacy, 178–80
Princess Diana, 27
prostitution, 9, 48
public schools, 72

rape, 8
'the rational male', 145
reactive relationships, 132–3,
    188
Reformation, 13, 47
Renaissance, 12–13
'repression', 81
rich, 28–9
roles, 136–7
Roman marriage, 1, 6–8, 192–3
Romantic marriage, 10–13, 45–6
Russia, 21, 62, 96

sacrament, 39
self-directed living, 43–4, 121–2,
    155, 161, 206
self-knowledge, 112, 129
separation, 73
serial monogamy, 26
sex, 30–1, 54–6, 80–4, 118–28,
    147–8, 207–8
sexual abuse, 69, 118
Shakespeare, W., 9, 46
shotgun marriage, 80
sin, 24, 112–4
singleness, 46, 77–91
slavery and family life, 8–9, 96–7
Sociobiology, 41
Sociobiology of Family, 18–20, 36,
    41
sphere sovereignty, 41–3
Something to Celebrate, 34, 218–9
statism, 39, 41–3, 195
Structuralism, 39
subsidiarity, 42
Sweden, 21

television, 25, 184, 215
theology, 217–9
time, 25, 100–1
Tournier, P., 138
transference, 66–7, 156–7, 184–5

trial marriage, 99–100
two-job marriage, 164–5, 167–70,
    172

unemployment, 29, 170–1
United States, 8, 21, 25, 62–3,
    95–7, 215, 219
universal man, 12
Updike, J., 216

Veblen, T., 16
Venus, 11, 13
Victorian values, 14–16
violence, 8–10, 137, 179
Virago, 13
Virgin Mary, 13

Wales, 28
Waley, A., 1
war, 7, 21, 61–3
wary woman, 95
wedding, 10, 39, 47, 100–1,
    116–17
Westermarck, E., 1, 18, 41
West, the, 18–19, 34, 47, 60, 91,
    166, 177, 214
Westernism, 7, 16, 22, 60, 80–2,
    98–9, 108–9, 122, 124, 142,
    164, 220–2
wholeness, 47, 133–5
wife control, 56, 58
wife-directed marriage, 44
wife-father relationship, 68–70
Wife of Bath, 149
withdrawal, 54, 137, 159
woman worship, 11–13
work, 10, 26, 29, 97–9, 142,
    164–73, 183, 210–11
working mother, 167–70
World War I, 61–2
World War II, 7, 21, 62–3
Young, M. and P. Willmott, 7–8